American Folk Art

Rug Hooking

*Folk Art Projects
with Rug-Hooking Basics,
Tips & Techniques*

LANDAUER BOOKS

American Folk Art

Rug Hooking

Copyright© 2005 by Landauer Corporation
Projects Copyright© 2005 by Barbara Carroll for the Woolley Fox®

This book was designed, produced, and published by Landauer Books
A division of Landauer Corporation
3100 NW 101st Street, Urbandale, IA 50322
800-557-2144; www.landauercorp.com

President/Publisher: Jeramy Lanigan Landauer
Director of Operations: Kitty Jacobson
Editor in Chief: Becky Johnston
Creative Director: Laurel Albright
Contributing Project Editor: Connie McCall
Contributing Technical Editor: Mary Helen Schiltz
Technical Illustrator: Linda Bender
Editorial Assistants: Debby Burgraff, Judy Hunsicker
Photographer: Craig Anderson Photography

Library of Congress Cataloging-in-Publication Data
Carroll, Barbara, 1940-
  Rug hooking : folk art projects with rug hooking basics, tips & techniques / [by Barbara Carroll].
        p. cm.
  ISBN 1-890621-92-7 (alk. paper)
1. Rugs, Hooked. I. Title: American folk art rug hooking. II. Title. TT850.C24 2005
746.7'4--dc22
                                2005051024

This book printed on acid-free paper.
Printed in China

10-9-8-7-6-5-4-3-2-1

ISBN 13: 978-1-890621-92-6
ISBN 10:   1-890621-92-7

From the Author

In January of 1987, Bobbie True and I made our way to Leawood, Kansas, to attend our very first rug hooking class with Emma Lou Lais—a story that has been lovingly retold many times. I certainly could not have known what a life-altering journey that would be.

It has been fun to watch my rug hooking progress from being able to use only five colors, to showing others how to use all of these textures that I love so much, and to teaching that purple trees are just fine and dandy and that there really are no rules except to hook from your heart.

I have so many memories, especially of three very good friends, teachers and mentors. These great ladies—Emma Lou Lais, Edyth O'Neill and Jule Marie Smith—have taught me and guided me to be the teacher and person I am today. Thank you all so much. So, ladies and gentlemen, smile when you hook, love your fellow rug-hooking friends, and remember that sharing is a gift from God.

Barb Carroll

Dedication

This book is dedicated to my wonderful friend Bobbie True, who is half my heart and soul. Without Bobbie my life would not be as full of love and not nearly as fun. Bobbie started me on this wonderful journey and has steadfastly stood by me with every step I have taken, never doubting that I could do each and every thing that came my way. Sometimes it was a "Hooray for you," sometimes a "Are you crazy??? but I know you can do it," and always with love in her heart. Thank you, Bobbie, with love and all of my heart.

Contents

Contents

Rug Hooking Projects

52

Rug Hooking Resources

122

Welcome to the Woolley Fox

During their 45 years of marriage, Wayne and Barbara Carroll have lived in various cities around the United States and have traveled the world. For their golden years, they wanted a place to hang their hats and roll out the welcome mat for friends and family—a place to call home. Twelve years ago the Carrolls found such a place in historic Ligonier, Pennsylvania. Barbara and Wayne snapped up the property and gave it the name *Woolley Fox* due to Barb's love for all things wool as a rug hooking enthusiast.

A rare, 100-year-old vintage wooden swan at the edge of the pool shares the view from the patio with Wayne and Barbara and their beloved family pets—Winston, a West Highland White, and Panda Bear, a black and white cat who enjoys the comforts of a rug designed by Bill Laraway and hooked by Jayne Hester.

Located on the edge of town, the 65-year old main house, shown below at dusk, is a former summer home built of stone from the property, with a post and beam porch. Also on the four-acre property are a guest house and the Woolley Cottage. The pond, a former swimming pool (above), is a refreshing summer-time treat filled with as many as 300 carp in a variety of colors. The cart (above left) is an antique.

Here and on the pages that follow, discover for yourself the old-world charm of the Woolley Fox grounds, cottages, and main house, all overflowing with Barb's extensive collection of old and new hooked rugs, many of them inspired by the antiques and collectibles that fill the house with warmth and comfort—truly a place to call home!

Welcome to the Woolley Fox

In recent years, the art of rug hooking has had a dramatic rise in popularity, creating demand for classes and for a source for wool and rug hooking supplies. Barb's expertise as a rug hooker and leading teacher made it apparent that the Woolley Fox was the ideal setting for displaying her growing collection of vintage hooked rugs and antiques, and for hosting classes and running a rug-hooking mail-order operation.

The Woolley Fox Cottage (above and at left), is a welcoming sight perched at the top of the hill above the winding drive that leads to the Woolley Fox. Visitors can sit for a spell on the front porch or take a short stroll down the path, passing a small, rare buckboard wagon along the way to the main house. The Woolley Fox is a gathering place where Wayne and Barbara Carroll share their gift for hospitality with visitors, friends and family alike. One of Barb's favorite folk art pieces, designed by a friend, is inscribed with a quote from the Roman poet Horace, "This corner of the earth smiles for me beyond all others."

Today, for the Carrolls, the Woolley Fox is a dream come true. With Wayne's help, Barb hosts as many as 20 mini-workshops each year at the Woolley Fox. The rug hookers who come eagerly anticipate such gatherings—especially in springtime. (For more about mini-workshops, resources and supplies for rug hooking, see page 143.)

A rustic red birdhouse, made by a friend out of recycled shingles from the guest house, offers a room with a view for bluebirds, cardinals, orioles, finch, and four varieties of woodpeckers. This penthouse-on-a-post overlooks a display of two of Barb's favorite rugs. The vintage rug with black cats (circa 1885), which usually hangs in the master bedroom, is a perfect companion piece for the hooked white cat duo designed by folk artist Warren Kimble (see page 90 for hooking instructions).

Barb's unique collection of old and new miniature log cabins is the decorating accent of choice for the impressive hooked rug (shown above and at left) that features a pictorial log cabin scene adapted from artwork by American folk artist Carol Endres.

The post-and-beam screened porch with flagstone floor and half-walls is home to replicas of log cabins, many made new to look old, and prized antiques such as the antique rocking horse (circa 1885), the cloth doll, and the rocker that was used as a prop in the filming of a PBS mini-series. Barb's ever-growing collection of antiques and collectibles is often the inspiration for the rugs she designs, such as Mollie's Star (right), which is hooked with wool colors that blend with vintage period pieces (see page 66 for hooking instructions), or for those she adapts for rug hooking from designs by leading artists.

Collections that have inspired many of Barb's hooked rugs are themed around sights common to early settlers, who used scraps of wool and burlap to create primitive hooked rugs. Bears from the forest, livestock penned by split-rail fence, stars and moon in the sky, and fruit such as strawberries, watermelon and pineapple (an early symbol of hospitality) were popular themes.

The rugs shown here demonstrate the versatality of a simple animal motif, such as a sheep, in rugs inspired by American folk art. The pictorial scene (at top), Watching Over Ewe, is adapted from artwork by Carol Endres (see page 58 for hooking instructions); the lamb hooked by Carole Virag is a Sandi Gore Evans design; and Flag Day Sheep (right) is Barb's original design (see page 98 for hooking instructions).

P atriotism—fromUncle Sam to the American flag—
is also a prominent theme in primitive folk art rugs. Barb's
collection of bears includes everything from a Boy Scout
bear sporting badges to a teddy boasting a "Roosevelt for
President" button. The folk-art Uncle Sam riding an eagle
(above) was adapted by Barb for rug hooking from artwork
designed by Sandi Gore Evans, and was hooked by Chris
Richey. Other patriotic designs by Sandi Gore Evans, the
flags and star (right), were adapted by Barb and hooked by
Bobbie True and Pat Klavuhn respectively.

  15—Welcome to the Woolley Fox

Barb teaches rug hooking for a design style she and a friend fondly call "Hannah"—the fictitious name for any design that resembles an old-style primitive hooked rug. The Hannah rug on the wall, (left) which was hooked by Barb, and the vintage horses from Barb's collection inspired *Debbie's Horse* (see page 82 for hooking instructions) and *Olde Horse* (below), hooked by Elaine Cathcart.

Bears, bears, bears and more bears! Barb just can't get enough of these furry friends, and she collects them by the dozen. Shown below are just a few of her favorites, along with a warm-your-heart teddy bear, Abraham, on a rug designed by Lori-Ann Baker-Corelis and hooked by Sue McCann.

$\mathbf{P}$ineapples, fruit, and berries frequently inspire appealing folk art. The pineapple rug (above left) is a Warren Kimble design hooked by Barbara Hill. An old maple sugar mold on the dining room wall inspired Barb's design of *Maple Sugar Hearts* (above right; see page 62 for hooking instructions). Complemented by the Nicholas Mosse "Landscape" dinnerware and by an antique water cooler, the *Two's Company* and *A Slice of Summer* rugs (below) are signature Warren Kimble, accented by braided borders (see pages 78 and 70 for hooking instructions).

Harvest has always been a special time of year for giving thanks for autumn's bounty. This season offers plenty of creative inspiration for American folk art rug hooking expression. *Mister Scarecrow* (left) is by Carol Endres; the owl and the jack-o'-lantern *Keeping Watch* (below) is by folk artist Warren Kimble (see pages 102 and 106 for hooking instructions).

Miniature rugs make great gifts, and they work up quickly for seasonal accents. The smiling jack-o'-lantern design by Sandi Gore Evans, an easy treat for Halloween, was hooked by Cindy Dillow.

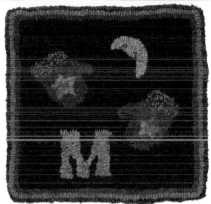

Warmth and welcome await guests at the Woolley Fox. Wayne and Barb often treat friends and family to holidays filled with collectibles, such as stuffed bears galore, the wheel from an old coffee grinder, and rugs like these. *Eight Is Enough* (top left) is designed by Warren Kimble, and *Frosty Friends* (lower left) is designed by Carol Endres (see pages 118 and 110 for hooking instructions). The rugs with stockings and mittens are a Sandi Gore Evans design, hooked by Kathy Ashcom and Pat Klavuhn, respectively.

Love of old-style collectibles led Barb to her true love—rug hooking. Nearly 20 years ago, Barb and her best friend Bobbie True "crashed" a rug hooking class led by an esteemed authority, Emma Lou Lais of Kansas City, Missouri, and the rest is history. Since then, Barb has co-authored two rug-hooking books with Emma Lou.

Rug hooking has become a family affair. The Carrolls' daughter Diane Lestina shares birthday cheer with Emma Lou Lais (above), the teacher whom Barb credits with sparking her interest in and subsequent love for American folk art rug hooking. With 80+ birthday candles on her cake, Emma Lou is still going strong.

One of Barb's favorite collectibles (right) is a wooden sheep, carved by Hal and Diane Denmead and named Emma in honor of Barb's friend and mentor.

Daughter Robin Carroll (below left) over-dyes all of Barb's wool. And Barb's granddaughters Abby Lestina and Molly Jensen (below center and right) have discovered rug hooking—learning the basics in one-on-one sessions with their favorite teacher!

Learning through sharing is a common theme in the rug hooking classes that Barb teaches throughout the year. Here, a group of students from several of her classes gather on the patio to enjoy the springtime sunshine and each others' company as they work on a variety of rug hooking projects in various stages of completion. Barb offers tips and pointers for techniques as students advance through projects that range from simple to challenging. Just arrived that day were new wools hand-dyed by Barb's daughter Robin Carroll, using the new dye formulas Barb developed especially for this book (see pages 30 and 31).

For the class wrap-up, students' rugs are lined up for a stunning show-and-tell.

Rug Hooking Basics

Sources of Wool

It is imperative to use good-quality wool. You can use new wool fabric just as it comes off the bolt, or old "recycled" wool from worn or out-of-date clothing, or even a worn-out woolen blanket. Be careful with blankets, however; make sure they are not too stiff and heavy.

Flannel Weight Wool

Flannel-weight wool, which is in jackets or plaid skirts, is most desirable for primitive rug hooking. A yard of 60" flannel-weight wool weighs about 12 ounces. If you use heavier wool, space out your loops more so the rug doesn't get crowded and bunch up. Gabardine and worsted wools are too thin and hard; please avoid these.

If you buy new "as-is" wool, look for 100 percent, or at least 80 percent, wool with no more than 20 percent man-made materials. If you are not sure about the content, there is a simple test. Pour a small amount of chlorine bleach into a glass container, put a small piece of fabric into the bleach, and let it stand. If the swatch dissolves overnight, the fabric is wool. If only a few threads are left, it is probably 80 percent wool and okay for hooking.

Recycled Wool

Finding "recycled" wool is something like a treasure hunt. Start with the family closet—yours first! If the family won't part with their treasures, it's off to the thrift store, a wonderful source of items that you can be sure the owner doesn't want any more. Yard sales are also a great place to find bargains. The best buys are skirts and slacks. They are easy to take apart, and you get the most wool for your money. Women's suits offer the skirt, plus some wool from the jacket.

The term "textured wool" refers to wool that has a pattern woven into it. Textured wools (see photo below) create a natural shading. They give depth to your rug, a greater interest, and a feeling of "time, light, and wear" that you see in the old rugs. Textured wool includes plaids, herringbone tweeds, checks, floral patterns, or even paisley.

Paisley is a fine wool woven with an intricate pattern.

"The look that paisley gives to a rug can't be duplicated with dyed fabric," says Cynthia Norwood, a friend who has incredible knowledge of the history of paisley.

Photo courtesy of Cynthia Norwood

Paisley Wool

According to Cynthia, paisley was made in several different textures. Weavers used the fleece of several kinds of sheep and sometimes they also incorporated silk. Paisleys from the 1870s and 1880s were often made with a lesser quality of wool, a difference you can feel.

Because paisley is thinner than most other wools, strips for rug hooking may need to be cut wider. Cynthia sometimes cuts them wide and then folds them in half lengthwise for more body.

Three projects in this book contain paisley: *Keeping Watch* (see page 106), *Maple Sugar Hearts* (see page 62), and *Debbie's Horse* (see page 82).

Cotswold and Merino

North Ronaldsay

North Ronaldsay and Jacob

Black Welch Mountain with white added in spinning

Cotswold mixed with undyed wool from other sheep

Black Badger-faced or Wern Ddu

Shetland: weft Jacob: warp

Black Welch Mountain with no white added

Jacob

Merino

Cotswold: warp Black Welch Mountain: weft

All Jacob colors

Merino

Jacob

Shetland: weft undyed Shetland: warp dyed

English wools courtesy of Richard Martin of Cotswold Woollen Weavers

Figuring Wool Amount

How much wool you need depends on your pattern and your hooking style. For primitive rug hooking, the general rule is that you need five to six times more wool than the area that the wool is to cover, so for a square foot of hooking you need 5 to 6 square feet of wool.

The main variable is how high you hook your loops. The old rule of thumb is to make your loops about as high as the width of the wool strips you are using, so you will need more wool if you hook very high. However, I teach that you should pull your loops to the height that is comfortable for you (see Forming Loops, page 40).

The practical way to see if you have enough wool is this: Fold the wool so you have six layers and place the stack over the part of the design where it will be used (at right, it is the center star). If the wool covers that part of the pattern, you have enough.

Rug hooking patterns typically list amounts of wool in ounces. A 36"-wide strip of 60"-wide wool off the bolt weighs about 12 ounces, and its area is 15 square feet or 2,160 square inches.

In the project instructions beginning on page 54, larger amounts of wool are given both in fractions of a yard and in ounces, like this:

For the star outline, third circle, and border outside the zigzag line, 1/6 yard (2 ounces). This is equivalent to a 6"-wide strip of 60"-wide yardage.

Smaller amounts of wool are given both in square inches and in a sample size to help you visualize the amount, like this:

For the background behind the star, 100 square inches (10" x 10"). Very small amounts are given as "several strips" or even "a few strips."

Mollie's Star (see page 66) is the "model" for the how-to illustrations, because it has several design elements common in primitive hooked rugs.

Mollie's Star *Hooked Rug*

Selecting Wool Colors

Choosing the colors is one of the most satisfying and fun parts of making a primitive rug. Even working from a pattern, for example *Mollie's Star*, is not simple paint-by-number.

Here are some tips that can help you make color decisions. Start by deciding whether you want a dark or light background. (A medium background gives a nice sense of age to the rug, but it is hard to color-plan around it.)

Choose an important color, something you like, either to use as the background or to draw the eye to a prominent motif in your design. As you choose other colors, try to have a "flow" of color, not "jumps" of color.

Put all the possible colors together on the floor. Some colors might look out of place. These are the ones to remove. But don't pull out too many; without variety and contrast, your rug will look muddy. Try scrunching up several wools together to see how they will look when they are hooked into the rug.

Mollie's Star *Wool Amounts*

As you choose colors for the objects in the design, remember there is nothing wrong with an olive green cat or a purple horse! Balance your colors within the design. Don't put all the reds on one side and all the blues on the other. Choose at least one color to use in a triangular arrangement to move the viewer's eyes around the rug.

And how about adding a touch of "spark" to your rug? Old rugs often had a spot of unexpected or unconventional color, probably something the rug hooker had on hand. This spark helps "lift" the rug so it doesn't just melt into the background.

Many rugs have at least one "definition line" between the background and the border, especially if the background and border are at all alike. This will be a contrasting color.

The border is a wonderful place to pick up colors from the central designs and give the rug a feel of continuity. You can even use a hit-or-miss approach, piling all your border strips into a heap and randomly pulling them out to use.

In *Mollie's Star*, the red of the star is carried out to the corners. The definition line is bright, and the border includes the blue. The orange is toned down by its complementary color, green (see Color Wheel on page 51). All the colors continue throughout the pattern, but the darkening towards the border emphasizes the red of the star.

Preparing Wool

Before you even begin cutting wool into strips, the wool must be washed, no matter where you got it.

When you wash your new wool, the fibers fill out a bit and the wool becomes softer. If there is any sizing (this is a glazing added to the surface of the fabric), it will wash out. Your nice new wool will be light, fluffy, and a pleasure to hook. If you don't pre-treat the yardage in this way, the finished rug will look cold, flat, and harsh.

Cut or tear the wool into one-yard pieces. Put the wool in the washing machine. Add 1/8 cup of Ivory® Liquid, and set the machine for a full wash, or a 20-minute cycle. A warm wash and a cold rinse is usually the best temperature setting. For thick wools, use a cold wash. For very thin wools, use one or even two hot wash cycles. After the wool is washed, dry it in the dryer on normal heat. Include a fabric-softening dryer sheet.

Sort recycled clothing into color piles. Do not take garments apart until after they have been washed and dried. Machine-wash related colors together in a warm Ivory Liquid wash and a cold rinse, as you do with new wool. Dry the clothing in a dryer with a big fluffy towel and a dryer sheet.

Basic Method for Dyeing

Note: You do not need to dye all your wool. The directions below are for when you want to change the color or shade of a piece of wool.

1. Soak the wool overnight in warm water with Ivory Liquid®. If you are dyeing a large amount of wool, soak the wool in the washing machine.

2. Wearing rubber gloves and an apron, follow the formula directions and mix the dyes in glass measuring cups, using a wire whisk.

3. Fill an enamel pot two-thirds full with water (about 6 to 8 quarts). Add the required amount of dye and 1 teaspoon of salt, and bring the mixture almost to a boil.

4. Add the soaked wool 1/2 yard (6 to 8 ounces) at a time. Turn the heat down to medium or medium-low and simmer the wool, stirring occasionally.

5. After 20 to 35 minutes, add about 1/3 cup of white vinegar. Stir and simmer for another 15 to 20 minutes or, for a darker color, about 30 to 40 minutes. Some very dark colors could take an hour. The wool absorbs the dye and the water clears; don't worry if it does not clear completely.

6. Remove the pot from the stove. Using tongs, carefully remove the wool and place it in the sink. Let it cool to room temperature.

7. Rinse the wool in the washing machine. Use the rinse cycle and spin-dry. Dry the wool in the dryer at medium heat, with a large towel.

Other Methods for Dyeing

Two specialized techniques for modifying the color of wools are "marrying" and "stewing." These often do not involve adding extra dye.

The "marrying" method

Imagine that you have three pieces of red-toned wool. One is an orange and red plaid, one is a cranberry herringbone, and one is a crayon-red check. All are red, but they don't quite go together. You would like to use them in your rug. What to do? "Marry" the colors.

To do this, soak the wool as if you were going to dye it. Fill a large enamel pot with water, and add a tablespoonful of Arm and Hammer washing soda or a detergent that does not contain bleach. Bring the water temperature up to medium high to dissolve the detergent. Add all the wet wools; they will bleed and share their colors with each other. You will have a wonderful potful of red water! Simmer the wool for 15 to 20 minutes, and add 1/4 to 1/3 cup of white vinegar. Continue to simmer the wool another 15 to 20 minutes, until the water has cleared. Let the wool cool in the pot, rinse, and dry it as you would after dyeing.

If you want varied shades from dark to light, start with the darkest wool in the pot. When the water is dark, add the vinegar. When the water is half as dark as it was, put a medium shade of wool into the pot. When the water is lighter still, again add a yet lighter shade. Simmer it all for about 15 minutes. Cool the wool, rinse it, and dry it. You should have dark, medium, and light shades of the original color.

The "stewing" method

"Stewing" is much like "marrying," but you use different colors of wool, to blend them. For example, you could stew lime greens, medium greens, and teal blues to get a color for grass. Or, you could take a bright yellow that is a bit too garish and stew it with a piece of purple.

To get a dirty-looking, antique background color, make a genuine stew of blue, red, green, purple, orange, and black.

Equipment for Dyeing

Dye pots, 12-quart size or larger if you are going to dye large pieces of wool, and preferably white enameled (not aluminum, which pits)

2-cup heatproof measuring cup

Non-iodized or kosher salt

White vinegar

Measuring spoons

Dye spoons (TOD spoons for measuring tiny amounts, available from Cushing's)

Stirring spoons or long-handled tongs

Notebook for record-keeping

Safety equipment: Apron, latex gloves, heavy rubber gloves, and dust mask

Cushing's Acid Dyes (Cushing's dyes are blended dyes with multiple color components)

Note: You should not use this equipment for food preparation; dyes make it unsafe.

Two additional aids you really should have are a Cushing's Colour Chart and a traditional color wheel, which shows shading from color to color and identifies complementary (opposite) colors.

Dyeing the Wool

New dye colors can be created by combining existing Cushing's Acid Dye colors. In cooperation with my daughter Robin Carroll and my friend Jayne Hester, I present seven brand-new colors.

The wools above were overdyed with my new dyes. Each recipe below tells how much of the mixed dye to use in a dye pot of simmering water.

Barb's Super Seven Dyes
O'Mally's Irish Green

1/2 teaspoon Hunter Green
1/2 teaspoon Myrtle Green
1/2 teaspoon Dark Green
1/2 teaspoon Bronze
1/16 teaspoon Plum
1/32 teaspoon Chartreuse

Mix these colors in 1 cup of boiling water.
Use 1/3 to 1/2 cup of dye formula.
Use over camels and beiges or light browns.

Hooker's Gold

1/2 teaspoon Bronze
1 teaspoon Old Gold
1/2 teaspoon Nugget Gold
3/32 teaspoon Plum

Mix these colors in 1 cup of boiling water.
Use 1/3 to 1/2 cup of dye formula.
Use over beiges, tans, or grays.

Ligonier Blue

1/2 teaspoon Blue
1/2 teaspoon Turquoise Blue
1/16 teaspoon Black
1/16 teaspoon Burgundy
1/16 teaspoon Khaki Drab

Mix these colors in 1 cup of boiling water. Use 1/3 to 1/2 cup of dye formula. Use over light grays and maybe medium-light grays.

Chuck's Orange

1/2 teaspoon Rust
1/4 teaspoon Orange
1/2 teaspoon Terra Cotta
1/4 teaspoon Medium Brown
1/16 teaspoon Blue

Mix these colors in 1 cup of boiling water.
Use 1/2 cup of dye formula.
Use over medium browns.

Jayne's Purple Poodle

1 teaspoon Violet
1/32 teaspoon Turquoise Blue
1/32 teaspoon Taupe

Mix these colors in 1 cup of boiling water.
Start off by using 1/2 cup of the mixed
formula, and go up as needed.
Use over light grays, light browns, and plaids.

Sampler Red

1 teaspoon Cardinal
1 teaspoon Egyptian Red
1/8 teaspoon Gold
1/8 teaspoon Old Gold
1/16 teaspoon Bronze Green
1/16 teaspoon Olive Green

Mix these colors in 1 cup of boiling water.
Use 3/4 cup of dye formula.
Use over beiges, camels, and light plaids.

Prentis House Red

1 teaspoon Terra Cotta
1 teaspoon Egyptian Red
1/2 teaspoon Dark Brown
1/8 teaspoon Bronze Green.

Mix these colors in 1 cup of boiling water.
Use 3/4 cup of dye formula.
Use over medium brown plaid.

Cutting Tools

Because rug hooking requires large amounts of very
narrow strips of wool, you need some way to cut the
wool into these strips.

Some people hand-cut
their wool, using the
Fiskars® spring-action
scissors in combination
with tearing the wool by hand.
This is fun to do, inexpensive, and
reminiscent of the way strips were cut for the
old-time primitive rugs.

Another fairly
inexpensive method
is to use a rotary
cutter with a
mat and a
quilter's ruler

Mechanical cutters make the job even easier. I recommend the Fraser 500-1 cutter and the Townsend cutter, both of which clamp onto the edge of a table. The Townsend is a heavy piece of equipment that has an easy-to-change blade cartridge; with the #8 blade, you cut three strips at once.

Fraser 500-1 on wooden clamp stand

Townsend on metal clamp stand

Two clamp-stands, one metal and one wooden, are welcome additions to my collection of tools. They both sit on the table and raise a clamp-on, long-handled cutter to a usable height without having to be attached to the table edge.

Cutting Techniques

Rug-hooking strips are referred to by numbers that represent strip width. Most of the sizes are stated in 1/32nds of an inch. For primitive rug-hooking, use these widths of strips:

#8 cut (8/32", which is 1/4")

#8.5 cut (10/32", which is 5/16")

#9 cut (12/32", which is 3/8")

#10 cut (1/2")

I advise beginners to work with a #8 or #8.5 cut. With experience, you can try slight width variations. The wider you cut the strips, the more texture you will see in your loops.

Cutting by Machine

When using textured wools, make sure that the wool stays strong and tight. Therefore it is crucial that you begin with a straight edge that's on-grain, parallel with either the warp (the lengthwise

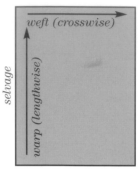

threads) or the weft (the crosswise threads) of the fabric. To keep the wool straight as you cut it, cut your strips on the grain of the wool.

Start by snipping through the fabric about 4" or 5" in from the selvage. Grasp both sides of the wool and pull the wool apart, tearing along the grain of the wool to get a manageable piece. A nice size to work with is a piece 6" or 8" wide and 12" to 18" long. Cut the yardage into pieces about the same size. Be aware that a strip that is off-grain is weaker and more difficult to hook.

Adjust the guide bar (see photo below) on your cutter. As you place the top edge (one of the short edges) of the wool in the cutter, make sure that it will feed straight through the cutter (see photo opposite, top). Steady it as it goes along. Set the strips aside after they are cut.

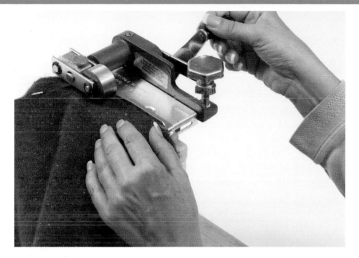

For the next cut, turn your wool end for end, and make the next cut from the bottom end. Then turn it once more and cut from the top end again. Alternating like this helps keep the strips on-grain. If you always cut from the same end, any slight crookedness adds up strip by strip, and the strips will curve.

Continue until the whole piece is cut into strips. If the strips do begin to curve, stop cutting the piece. Snip through the edge of the fabric again, and make a fresh tear. Cut as many strips as you expect to need.

Cutting with a Rotary

You can also use a rotary cutter, along with a self-healing mat and an 18-inch Plexiglas™ ruler (a quilter's ruler). Using a rotary cutter requires some hand strength to hold the ruler firmly in place. Again, make sure you cut right on the grain, to keep the pieces straight.

To square it up, snip the edge of the wool near the selvage and parallel to the selvage. Grasp both sides of the cut and pull the wool apart, tearing along the grain of the wool. This leaves a nice, on-grain edge. Snip and tear the wool again to get

a piece of a manageable size. A nice size to work with is a piece 6" or 8" wide and 12" to 18" long.

Lay the wool on the mat, and place the ruler, right side up, near the edge of the wool. On the ruler, identify a lengthwise line for the strip width you want. For example, if you want a #8 cut, that is equal to a 1/4" width, so locate the 1/4" line on the ruler.

Move the ruler so the 1/4" line is aligned along the torn edge of the wool and the edge of the ruler is on the wool, positioned to be a cutting guide.

Place one hand (your "holding" hand) on the ruler, fingers spread out along the ruler, parallel to the place where you are going to start cutting. Arch your hand so that only the finger tips and the top of your thumb are touching the ruler. Lean forward to put some weight on the ruler, but don't lean too hard; the ruler can shift and slide around with either too little or too much weight on it.

Release the protective cover on the rotary cutter. Run the blade along the edge of the ruler, using a fluid motion. Always cut away from your body. As you move the rotary blade along the wool, "walk" your hand along the ruler. That is, bring your thumb up to your fingers, keep your thumb solidly in position, and shift your fingers forward a few inches. Keep your hand parallel to the rotary blade.

Continue cutting wool strips. After every five or six cuts, turn the wool end for end so you start from the other end of the piece.

Cutting by Hand

If I need only a small amount of one color, I like to hand-cut the wool with spring-loaded Fiskar® scissors, which are much easier on your hand than regular scissors. Again, make sure that the wool is cut straight.

You can cut all the strips with the scissors, or you can follow the cut-and-tear method, using scissors to cut a strip of wool about an inch wide and then just tearing it down the middle by hand.

Choosing a Backing

A good backing is the foundation of a good rug. In the past, it was often the burlap backing that wore out, long before the rug itself aged. Today's rugs are hooked on much better foundation fabric, so you can expect your rug to last a long time.

When you hook a rug, you pull strips of wool up through the weave of the backing on which your pattern is drawn. Several fabrics can be used for backing, but I recommend only two of them, monk's cloth and primitive linen. Both can accommodate the wider strips that are used in primitive rugs. Monk's cloth and primitive linen are the only backings used for the patterns sold by Woolley Fox.

Monk's cloth is an evenly woven backing made of 100 percent heavy cotton. It is soft and pliable and easy to hook on. It comes in natural and is available in several widths.

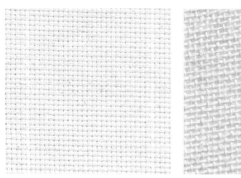

Monk's Cloth   *Primitive Linen*

Primitive linen is not the same thing as the usual linen sold in fabric stores. Primitive linen has a more open weave. Unlike the old burlaps that rotted away, linen actually is stronger when it is wet. It is considered to be the longest-lasting backing for hooked rugs.

You need to use a piece of backing that is 8" longer and 8" wider than the finished size of the rug, at the minimum. That means that if your design is 18" by 30", the backing must be a minimum 26" by 38", to leave at least a 4" margin all around. You will eventually trim off the excess, but you need that margin to hold the backing securely on the frame.

To prevent fraying and raveling, serge the backing all around the edges, or use a zigzag stitch all around. And if you do not have a sewing machine, you can fold wide masking tape around the edges. You will cut away the tape when you trim the backing as part of finishing the rug.

Choosing the Design

You can draw your own design, freehand or with templates cut from cardboard or plastic. Draw the full-size design on paper first, not directly onto the backing.

If you purchase a pattern from a supplier like the Woolley Fox, the design usually comes printed on a good backing fabric. If you use a design from this book, the patterns are drawn to scale on a grid and need to be enlarged before you can transfer them to the backing. Many copy centers have an extra-large copier that you can use, or you can enlarge the grid yourself and then hand-copy the design.

Preparing the Backing

Cut the backing 8" longer and 8" wider than the finished size of the rug. Establish the edge of the rug on all four sides. On all four edges, measure in about 4" to mark the edge of the rug. Make sure that the edge of the rug runs perfectly straight along the grain of the weave of the backing. Use a ball-point pen to run along the groove between the threads. Turn the backing as you work so you are pulling the pen toward you for each line, holding the backing taut with your other hand.

If there are other border lines, repeat the process for each of them, keeping them straight on the weave. This is the only part of the rug that needs to be perfect!

To prevent fraying, stay-stitch the backing about 1" from the edge of your design with serging, zigzag, or a couple rounds of straight stitching.

Transferring the Design

To transfer the design to the backing, you will need a ball-point pen, a fine-point Sharpie permanent marker, a metal ruler, and a tracing medium, such as Red Dot Tracer™. Red Dot is a transparent fiber cloth that has a grid of pale red dots printed on it at 1" intervals. It's great because the evenly spaced red dots help you make straight lines. You can also use another similar tracing product or nylon (not polyester) organdy. Some rug hookers use nylon netting or screen.

Place the full-size design, right side up, on a flat surface that is large enough for the entire design so you don't have to shift the design while you are tracing it. A dining room table with a protective pad is ideal. Lay the Red Dot on top of the paper design. Smooth the Red Dot and pin it to the corners of the design.

With the Sharpie, trace over your drawing to transfer it to the Red Dot (see photo below). Start

at the center of the design so you don't get ink on your hands. Don't try to draw with one continuous line. Use a ruler and the red dots to make straight lines. When you finish, remove the pins and pick up the Red Dot and the paper design.

Lay your prepared backing flat on the table, and center the Red Dot on top of it so the edges of the design are along the pen lines on the backing.

Using the Sharpie, make a dot at each corner of the design. The ink bleeds through the Red Dot and onto the backing. Pressing lightly, transfer any straight lines onto the backing, and then trace the rest of the design to transfer it. Don't press too hard on the marker, or the lines on the backing will bleed.

Remove the Red Dot. The marker lines will be a little light (see photo below). Go over them again with the marker.

Switch to the ball-point pen, and use the grooves in the weave to draw straight lines between the corner dots on the backing. Go back to the marker and trace over the straight lines. Use a ruler because the marker is too thick to go into the grooves of the weave.

The Frame

Choosing a Frame

One piece of equipment that you really need is something to hold your pattern taut.

If you want to try hooking a small project without purchasing much equipment, you can hook with the backing inserted into an embroidery or quilting hoop.

Commercial frames come in several types and sizes. Some are collapsible, some are on floor stands, some tilt, and others are stationary frames you hold on your lap. Most frames have carding strips, which are little metal gripping fingers that extend along the sides all the way to the corners.

I love the Morton Frame that sits on my lap. Its carding strips grip the backing

Morton Frame

really well to keep my work from slipping. The level frame swivels 360 degrees so you can turn your work while the base stays in place. The frame I use is only 9" by 11", but I have used it to work on rugs as large as 30" by 58". Other frames are available in 10" by 20", in 14" by 16", and in 20" by 20" for a floor stand.

Attaching the Pattern

1. Starting with the top of the frame, position the pattern (backing) so the area where you want to begin will be in the center of the frame.

2. To make sure the pattern is fixed to the carding strip, grasp the pattern at both sides of the front edge, pull the pattern taut, and tug it down over the frame. The carding strips should really grab the pattern.

3. Tug gently on the backing to stretch the pattern evenly over the edges of the frame.

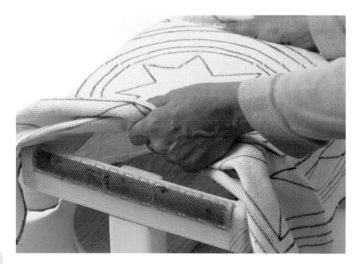

Hooks

When pioneer women hooked rugs for their homes, they had to make do with simple tools, often homemade. Hooks were a bent nail inserted into a handle. Now there is a variety of hooks to choose from, in all shapes, sizes, and prices.

The rug hook is a sturdy steel shank, one end hooked and the other end inserted into a wooden handle. Unlike a latch hook, the rug hook has no moving parts. The handle must fit your hand comfortably and the shank must be thick enough to open up the weave of the backing to pull the wool strip up through the backing in a loop.

For primitive-rug hookers, I usually recommend the Ritchie or Hartman hooks.

For my own hooking, I use only two hooks, and I use both of them all the time. One is a Ritchie Dale's Easy Grip hook made in England, and the other is a Hartman Primitive hook with an Ergo handle.

Ritchie Dale's Easy Grip Hook

Hartman Primitive Hook

Their handles differ and your hand placement is a little different on each. I switch between them to reduce the risk of carpal tunnel syndrome, which can be caused by repetitive motion. Both hooks have a nice big shank that opens the backing easily and that also makes a fluffier loop.

If you are just starting out, start with a hook that has a large shank for the projects in this book. As you become more experienced, you can try other hooks.

Tools & Scissors

There are several general sewing tools you should keep handy while you are hooking your rug.

Besides the specialized scissors, rotary cutter, or machine that you use for cutting the wool strips, there are a couple other cutting aids that are useful. Use small knife-edge or appliqué scissors for little chores, such as trimming the "tails" (the ends of the strips) so that your loops and tails are all the same height, and regular sewing shears for general use, such as trimming the backing when the rug is finished.

Tools needed for finishing the rug include a hand-sewing needle and a jumbo bent tapestry needle known as a gold needle. A metal ruler is also a useful tool to keep at hand.

Knife-Edge Appliqué Scissors

Storage

Where to stow all this? An easy solution is an assortment of baskets in several sizes for miscellany, wool strips currently in use, and wool strips that remain from previous projects.

Hooking the Rug

Beginning Hooking

The art of rug hooking brings together so many aspects of design and color and creativity. In a sense, it is painting a picture with the wool and the texture of the wool.

The actual hooking is the process of pulling strips of wool through a backing with a hook so they form consecutive loops on the surface of a backing.

There are many variations in how experienced rug hookers work. For example, some people do not turn their frames, but I simply cannot hook without turning the frame.

There truly is no right or wrong here. I teach and hook by the "no rules" method. Play with the wool, have fun, and do not worry about rules and what needs to be what color.

Ten Tips Before You Start

- *If you are right-handed, you will hook from right to left, rolling your hook to the right; you will hook from up to down. If you are left-handed, you will hook from left to right, rolling your hook to the left; you will still hook from up to down.*

- *Start in the center of the backing and work towards the outside.*

- *Insert the hook into every second or third hole, not every hole.*

- *The old rule of thumb is that each loop should be about as high as the wool strip is wide. Pull your loops to the height you are comfortable with!*

- *When you come to the end of a strip of wool, finish that strip and start the next one in the same hole.*

- *Outline an object just inside the drawn black lines, and then fill it in.*

- *Don't drag a strip from one place to another under the rug. Clip it off and start fresh.*

- *Be careful not to twist strips.*

- *From row to row, stagger the starting and stopping points. The loops will act like a zipper, fitting into each other.*

- *Hook along the contour of objects, following their shape.*

Forming Loops

With the pattern (backing) firmly in place on your frame, you are ready to hook. Take a deep breath; you are now starting on a fabulous journey.

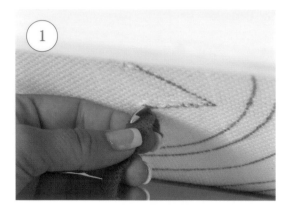

A. Hold the wooden handle of the hook in the palm of your right hand, with your forefinger slightly extended toward the metal shank and with the hook pointing up.

B. Underneath the pattern, hold the wool strip with your left hand, between thumb and forefinger. (If you are left-handed, just reverse these directions.)

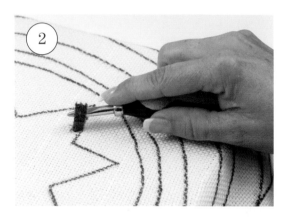

C. Choose a starting point. Usually this is in the middle of the pattern. You will be hooking either from right to left or from up to down. Insert the hook down through the pattern. As it goes through to the underside, the hook should just barely touch the left thumb and forefinger (see photo 1).

D. Catch one end of the wool strip with the hook and pull it up through the hole (see photo 2). This is the "tail"; pull it up at least 1" (you will clip it later). All the tails, both beginning and ending, will be on the top. The hooking will feel smooth under the backing.

E. To make your first real loop, push the hook down through the very next hole, and catch the wool. Bring the wool up to the top, and roll the hook (with the wool loop) back towards your right (see photo 3). This keeps the loops even and makes a fluffy loop. Make the loop a height that is comfortable for you.

F. To make your second loop, skip to the second or third hole in the backing (see photo 4). If you hook in every hole, your hooking will be too tight and your rug will buckle. Repeat this procedure until you come to the end of the strip. Try to make the loops even, all very nearly the same height.

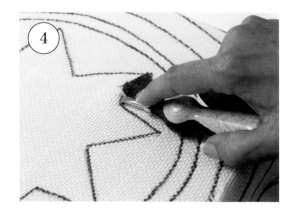

G. Bring the end of the strip (the "tail") up in the hole right next to the last loop you made (see photo 5).

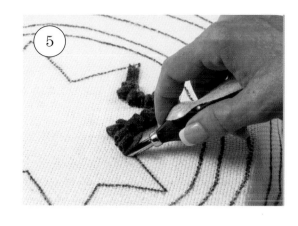

H. To start the next strip, bring its beginning tail up in the exact same hole as the end tail from the first strip, and then continue hooking loops (see photo 6).

I. If you are new to hooking, use your Sharpie marker to draw a line, a "comfort line," where the second row should go before you start hooking it (see photo 7).

J. When you start a new row, don't begin it right under the first row. Stagger the starting points of rows. The loops should be close but not too close. They should just touch shoulders, not hug (see photo 8)!

Barb's First Rug

With my first rug, I hooked it way too tight. I hooked in almost every hole. It was so tight, it wouldn't press out. To get my last loops in, I had to use a hammer on the edge of my hook. But now I laugh and tell people, It's a Noah's Ark! The water is supposed to ripple!

My second rug was my favorite because I could sit and look at my first, and see that I'd actually finished a rug. Besides, I could avoid repeating some of my mistakes!

You should always enjoy your first rug, no matter what mistakes you think you made, because if you didn't hook that rug, then you wouldn't have begun your rug-hooking journey.

A snippet basket gathers leftover pieces of wool strips. This, and other baskets are made by Sherry Sayles.

Hooking Points on a Star

Stars are fun. They can create a whimsical feel to areas of your rug. You can hook them in multiple wools, or you can outline and fill them with just one wool. Many stars have rounded points. Hook those by following the shape of the star, giving it a very primitive look.

However, if your pattern has a star with sharp points, here is an easy way to achieve the look you want.

1. Start hooking the outline of the star about halfway up one of the arms (see photo 1).

2. Make sure that you hook just inside the line (see photo 2).

3. When you get to the point, rotate your frame and hook a loop exactly on the point (see photo 3).

4. Turn your frame again, and continue hooking to the next arm, remembering to stay just inside the line (see photo 4).

Follow this procedure on each of the other points. By rotating the frame to your left, you change the direction of the loop; this creates a sharp point. Remember to follow the shape of the star when you fill it in.

For sharp points on quarter moons or triangles, follow this same procedure. Always make sure you hook exactly on the point, and then turn your frame so the loops will go in a different direction.

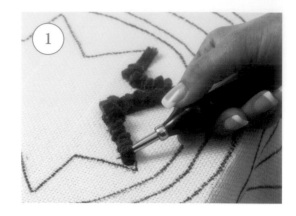

Hooking a Circle

Circles are easy if you start from the outside and work toward the center. "Outline and fill" is the general rule. Start by outlining the circle and then fill it row by row (see photo 1). Here is one place where you might end up with just one single tail in a hole. That will be in the very center of the circle and will be no problem.

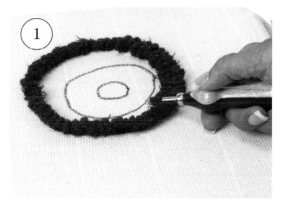

Do you want your circle to have a more primitive appearance? Start from the center and work outward (see photo 2). This leaves an uneven outer edge. You can even start slightly off-center for a look that's fun and unusual.

As my friend and first teacher Emma Lou Lais says, "For primitive rug hooking, imperfect is perfect!"

Hooking a Definition Line

For most rugs, a definition line is a good idea. This is a row hooked exactly on the line for the border, and you hook it before you start hooking either the border or the background. The definition line contains the background hooking and keeps that area looking crisp (see photo 3).

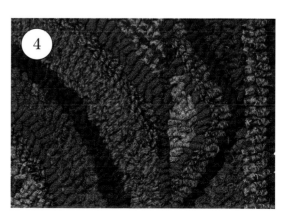

A definition line adds a spark of color and helps unify the design, especially if you pick up an important color from the design (see photo 4). Usually this should be a color that contrasts with the border and background. However, that is not a hard and fast rule. Some rugs do not need a different wool between the background and the border. Make the corners square just as you would for the border itself.

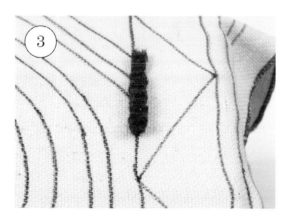

Hooking the Background

Backgrounds are a great place to have some fun hooking in swirls and random curves.

You should have already hooked the definition line, to contain the background hooking near the border. To contain the background hooking in the rest of the rug, it is also usually wise to hook one row of background wool around each motif (design element) that stands out against the background. If you are using a mix of several wools in your background, just mix them up as you hook around the motifs.

There are several ways to hook backgrounds.

The "grass/sky" method

Hook movement lines in the grass area, sort of like slopes or small hills. You then hook the grass by following these lines so that the grass area has a gentle slope or sway to it. For the sky, you use what I call the "lazy S" method. Turn your rug sideways and draw very lazy S lines in the sky area. Exaggerate these lines so they are shallow and long. Now hook these lines with your "sky" wool, and then just follow that shape as you hook the sky. This creates a very soft and wavy look (see photo 1).

The "swirl" or "web" method

Hook around all the motifs once or twice, and then use a Sharpie pen to draw on your background, drawing either swirls or a series of irregularly shaped areas. Following the shapes of these areas, hook on the lines and then just continue to fill in the shape until that area is entirely hooked. This creates an interesting background with nice movement in it. If you are using more than one wool, mix the wools randomly (see photo 2).

The "old rug" method

Another fun method is to section your background and hook each section in a different direction (see photo 3).

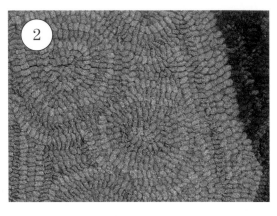

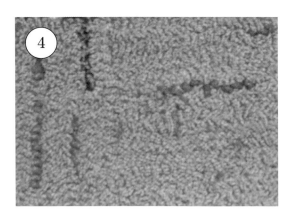

The "horizontal" method

For a different look, you can hook the entire background horizontally, using several wools that are close in color value. Horizontal hooking also works when you are hooking a large animal, say a nice big sheep. Hook your sheep in a fairly quiet texture and then "hit or miss" the horizontal background, using left over strips from other rugs (see photo 4).

An "aging" technique

It's lots of fun to "age" your rug by hooking patches or stains into the background. Many old rugs were patched to repair areas that were worn or damaged. The wool in the patch rarely matches the original wool. To simulate the patched look, section off an area or two in the background and hook those spots in closely-colored wool. To simulate a stain, choose a wool that is just a shade darker than the original (see photo 5).

Whatever background method you choose, remember to have fun with your rug.

Hooking the Border

There are several ways you can hook a border. Often, I work the outermost line around all four sides before proceeding to the next line, just inside the first. Other times I hook the rows of the border in a different order, working the first row on one side, the second row on that same side, and so on until that side is complete, and then pivoting the frame and starting on the next side. In any case, establish your outside lines first, to help you keep the rows straight.

Colors for the border should pick up the colors in the rug design. Sometimes the just-right choice will be a plaid that combines several of the colors. Sometimes hooking in a hit-or-miss fashion works well, using randomly selected strips of the colors that are in the rug. It does not matter much where you start hooking your border.

Hooking Square Corners

Square corners in a border look great, and they add a neat and finished appearance to your rug.

With a pen and a ruler, draw a line from the corner of the inner line of the border, through the border, to the corner of the outer line of the border.

Now take your border wool and hook down toward you. When you reach the drawn line, hook a loop exactly on that line.

Then rotate your frame to change the direction of the loops, hook a loop on the line again, and continue to hook toward yourself. The corner will actually be mitered.

Cotton binding tape: This is a 1-1/4"-wide tape that comes in many colors. Try to match the color of your border wool. Binding tape is sold at rug-hooking specialty shops and is also available by mail order.

Tapestry yarn: I use Paternayan three-ply tapestry yarn. A strand of Paternayan tapestry yarn is made up of three plies of wool. Strands are usually precut in lengths of about 33". In this book, the directions for each of the rugs give an approximate number of strands for the binding. Each 33" strand of yarn binds 2" to 3" of the rug. Choose tapestry yarns that are the same colors as your border wool.

Materials for Finishing

A whipped edge (see photo 4, opposite) is a beautiful finishing touch to a rug. If you match colors nicely, the whipping not only finishes the rug but also makes a lovely frame. It's a bit time-consuming, but definitely a worthwhile process!

To finish a rug you will need cotton binding tape and tapestry yarn.

Clover gold bent-point tapestry needle

Quilting thread

Using Tapestry Yarn

Because the tapestry yarn is three-ply, you can customize its color by separating the plies and re-combining them to reflect the colors in your border.

For example, sometimes my border wool is fairly simple, maybe a herringbone with just two colors. Then I would choose two tapestry yarns in those colors, say black and beige. If the dominant color is black, I would separate and reassemble the strands with two plies of black and one of beige. Now, if I have a very busy plaid of, say, red, gold, blue, and brown, then I would choose three of the colors, pull the strands of yarn apart, and put them back together with one ply of each of the three colors. This is not my favorite thing to do, but it looks great when your rug is finished.

A   Begin by trimming the backing to a little less than 1" from your last row of hooking, to make sure that when you are finished with the binding process, your trimmed backing will lie under the binding tape.

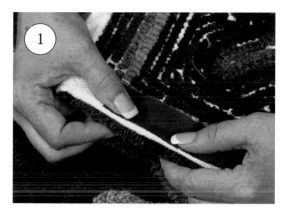

B. You need enough binding tape to go around the perimeter of your rug, plus about another 5". (Wash this cotton tape before you use it, so that it is pre-shrunk when you bind the rug.) Now lay your cotton binding tape at the edge of your fold and, bringing the needle towards you, enter the binding tape about 1/4" from the top. Bring the needle through the binding tape, back towards the last row of loops.

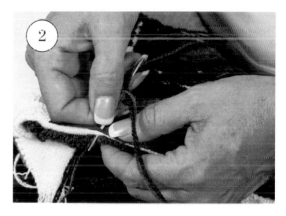

C. Now fold the backing toward the wrong side of your rug; use the outermost edge of your loops for your guide. If you like, you can lightly press the fold line (see photo 1).

D. Start about 2" from a corner or any place you like; however, starting on a corner is not recommended. Thread your gold needle with tapestry yarn; do not knot the end of the yarn. Start underneath your fold and push the needle up to the top of your work area, close to the last row of loops (see photo 2).

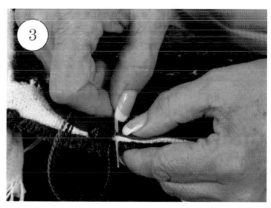

E. You will be working from right to left. What you are doing is "wrapping" the yarn around the fold and the top of the binding tape to create a whipped edge. Continue to "wrap" around the rug. Each time you insert the needle, make sure the yarn lies next to the previous stitch but does not overlap it (see photo 3). Do not pull the yarn too tight, or the edge of the rug will become uneven and will curl.

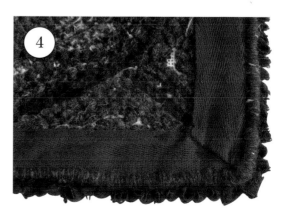

F. When you reach a corner, fold the tape on the next side down over the tape on the side you have been working on, and continue on around the corner, back to your starting place.

G. Now thread the hand-sewing needle with quilting thread, and just tack down the binding with a running stitch (see photo 4 for a look at the finished back of *Mollie's Star*).

Adding a Braided Border

Select wools that complement the colors in your rug, possibly even the same wools that you used in the rug.

How much wool will you need? This is where some guesswork comes in. There are many variables in the process—how thick the wool is, how tightly you braid, and how much you ease the braid onto the rug. For example, *A Slice of Summer* (see photo 1 and page 70) took 15" of 2"-wide wool for each of the three strands to create a finished, braided length of 12".

This is only a guideline to help you approximate how much wool you will need. If you need more, you can add more right up until you finish.

Making the Braid

A. Cut the wool into 2"-wide strips. Sew the strips of each color together end to end to create three strips of equal length. Press all the joining seams open, using a steam iron.

B. On each of the three long strips, fold the two long edges in 1/2" toward the center so the raw edges just meet in the center, and steam press the strips again. The wool strips now measure 1" in width (see photo 2).

C. Fold each strip in half the long way so the edges meet on one side and there is a fold on the other edge. Use the sewing machine to stitch the length of each strip close to the open edge (see photo 3).

D. When all three strands are complete, you are ready to start braiding. Use a large safety pin or clamp to hold the ends of all three strands together. Find a nice snug-fitting drawer, slip the pinned section into the drawer, and close the drawer.

E. Braid the strands in the traditional manner, just like pigtails. When you get to the end, use another large safety pin to hold the final ends together (see photo 4). The braid is now ready to be applied to your hooked rug .

Applying the Braid

A. On the backing of the finished rug, use a pen to draw a 2" border all around, measuring from very close to the hooking. Sew a line of zigzag stitching just inside the line, and trim off the excess backing.

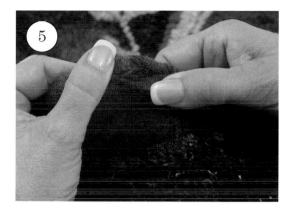

B. Leaving 1/2" of the backing to form a lip edge on the right side of the rug, fold the remaining backing to the wrong side of the rug and baste it in place all around the rug.

C. To apply the braid, begin by placing one pinned end of the braid very close along the edge of the hooking, on top of the lip you created. Stay as close to the hooking as possible so the backing will not show when you finish applying the braid. Start in an area that is away from any corner and not central to the focal point of the rug. Leave 3" to 4" of braid free to work with when you come back around to end the border, and begin basting the braid to the lip along the edge of the hooking. Ease the braid in gently all the way around the rug, especially at the corners. Do not pull on the braid.

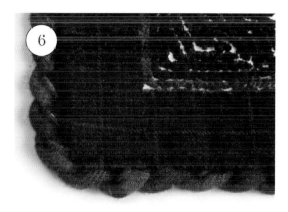

D. When you reach the end, cut the strands of braiding and work them into the strands from the beginning section. When you are pleased with the blending, stitch where necessary to anchor the ends together (see photo 5). Each rug ends differently, so plan before you cut.

E. Go back and hand-sew the entire braid in place with more permanent stitching. On the back of the rug, you can apply cotton binding tape to cover the rug backing, or you can use strips of wool in a coordinated color (see photo 6).

Pressing the Rug

Hooray! You have finished hooking your rug. Feels good, doesn't it? Now, off to the ironing room.

1. Lay your rug, right side down, on a hard surface, your ironing board if the rug fits or the floor if the rug is large. I usually do the pressing on the vinyl floor of my studio.

2. Lay a damp terry towel on the backing of the rug, and with a hot iron, press the towel that is on the rug (see photo below). DO NOT IRON IT. Just lay the iron on the towel, press, and then pick up the iron and move to the next spot. Continue this process until you have pressed the entire back of your rug.

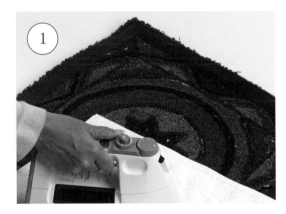

3. Flip the rug over, right side up, and repeat the process. Let it dry overnight on the flat surface.

Caring for Your Rug

To display your rug on a wall, use a dowel rod. If your new rug is to go on the floor, it should have a pad. Remember that the rug is made of little loops; try to protect it from pet claws and boot cleats.

When you need to take a rug somewhere or to store it, always roll it with the top side out. Never fold a hooked rug or roll it inside out, either of which could cause the backing to break down and weaken the foundation of your rug.

I have many hooked rugs on the floors of my home and also display a lot of rugs on the walls. All of them are vacuumed regularly, using a canister or hand-held vacuum, not an upright, especially not an upright that has a beater action.

If you live where there is snow, look for a winter day when the snow is very dry and fluffy. Take your rug outside and lay it facedown on the snow. This does a lovely job of brightening and cleaning the rug. If there is no snow, spray the rug with a dry carpet cleaner, and sweep or vacuum it off.

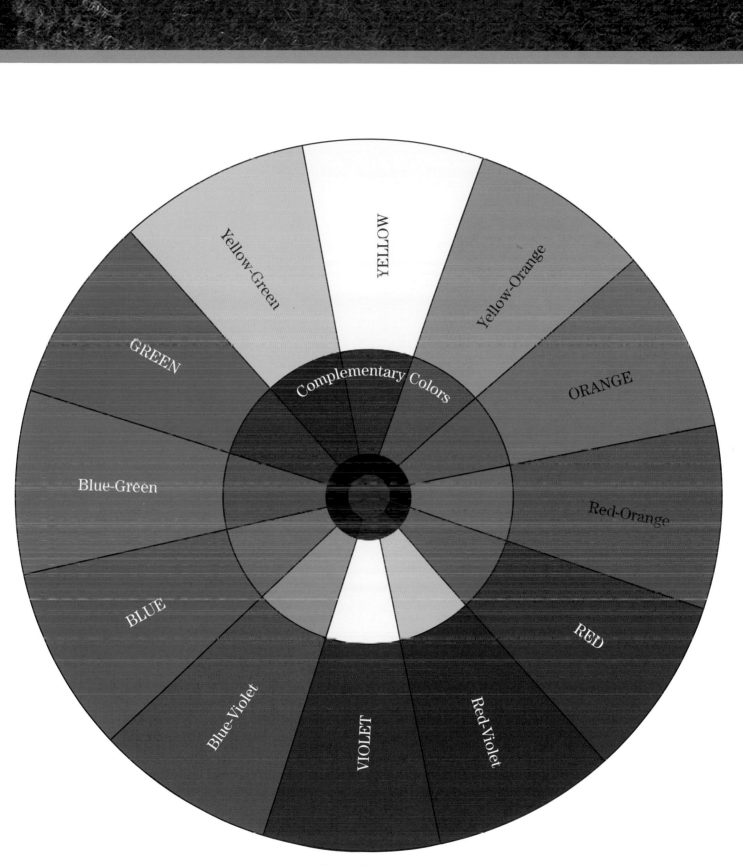

YELLOW

Yellow-Orange

ORANGE

Red-Orange

RED

Red-Violet

VIOLET

Blue-Violet

BLUE

Blue-Green

GREEN

Yellow-Green

Complementary Colors

Color Wheel

Rug Hooking Projects

July Cabin

A whimsical rug! The trees in the pots with flags on the branches make absolutely no sense, but really add to the fun of the rug.

—Barb

July Cabin
Artwork by Carol Endres

Rug design by Barbara Carroll
Hooked by Sue McCann

The art of rug hooking flourished during America's colonial days when artists were inspired primarily by their surroundings and imagination. American folk art was primitive with unusual combinations of motifs—often out of perspective but usually balanced. Adapted from artwork by Carol Endres, the imaginative elements in the *July Cabin* rug (sheep half the size of the cabin and flags waving out of enormous trees in tiny pots) still maintain a sense of balance.

Refer to the photograph of the finished rug to guide your choice of wool colors.

Logs hooked in a brown wool would simply fall into the background. So the logs are red, and they create a cheery rug. The windows are a soft tweed.

Because of the medium background and dark chimney, you need a bright wool to bring the cat forward to the viewer's eye.

How to make such small flags look like they should? A variety of blue checks in the cantons and a variety of herringbones in red-and-cream or red-and-gray help the flags look right.

The two sheep are hooked with dark wools. At first glance they look the same, both black, but they are not. The left-hand sheep is hooked with a blue herringbone, and the right-hand sheep is hooked in a dark blue and green check; its legs are dark green. Subtleties like this move your rug a step up from the ordinary.

Green leaves would have been almost impossible to see, so they're purple leaves. Think fun in your rugs!

The four rows of the outer border are of a great soft plaid that picks up the colors from the rug.

Turquoise for the door is light-hearted and fun.

Learning the Basics

Before you begin, refer to Rug Hooking Basics, pages 22–51, a complete guide to selecting, dyeing and cutting the wool; transferring the design to the background; gathering materials and supplies; hooking the rug; and finishing and caring for your rug. You'll find materials for the rug motifs, background, border, and binding listed below.

For the sheep
- 100 square inches (10" x 10") for the bodies
- Several strips for faces and legs

For the flag trees and pots
- 180 square inches (10" x 18") total for the flags
- 120 square inches (10" x 12") for the tree trunks
- Several strips for the leaves
- 75 square inches (15" x 5") for the pots
- Strips for the rims of the pots

For the house
- 1/6 yard (2 ounces) total for logs, windows, door, and chimneys
- 150 square inches (10" x 15") for the roof
- 60 square inches (10" x 6") for the smoke

For the moon
- 25 square inches (5" x 5")

For the stars
- 35 square inches (5" x 7")

For the cat
- Several strips of bright wool
- Narrow dark strip for whiskers and eyes

For the background
- 2-1/3 yards (32 ounces) total, a lighter and a darker wool

For the border
- 5/6 yard (10 ounces) total for 2 rows of liner and 4 rows of border

For the binding
- 14 feet of cotton binding tape, pre-washed
- 55 strands of 3-ply tapestry yarn

Hooking the Rug

Finished size: 25" x 47"
Size 8.5 cut

Skill Level: ★ ★ ★ ★

1. Start with the house. Outline the windows, hook the crossbars, and outline the door. Fill in the window areas and the door. Outline the sides and bottom of the house. Hook the chinking between the logs, and then hook the logs, all horizontally.

2. Outline the roof and use the same wool to hook the vertical lines in the roof. Fill in the roof, hooking in vertical rows. Hook the cat, using a narrow strip of dark wool for the whiskers and for the eyes, which you can do just up, up, and clip. Hook the chimneys (again, outline and fill), being careful not to lose the cat's tail. Use two different wools for the chimney, and use vertical rows to hook the smoke.

Tip: Notice the special touch created by the wonderful purple and gray bouclé in the smoke.

3. Hook the flag trees and pots next. Making sure you hook just inside the lines, hook just one row of gold for the rims of the pots. Outline and fill the rest of each pot. Hook the stem next, and then outline and fill the leaves.

Tip: Hooking just inside the lines is crucial at this point; otherwise, the pots and flags will become much too large for the design.

For a stars-and-stripes look, choose a blue checked wool for the canton and a red-and-cream or red-and-gray wool for each flag, and hook the flags.

4. Hook the sheep using two different body wools. Start by hooking the face and ear first (you do not need to hook eyes), using a very dark wool, and then outline and fill the body of the sheep Hook the legs, just one row for each leg.

5. Hook the stars now. Outline and fill them, following the star shape and making sure you stay just inside the lines. To make sharp points on the stars, follow the directions on page 42. Hook the moon next; again, keep the points sharp.

6. Hook the line between the border and the background. This will contain your hooking while you fill in the background. Hook around all the motifs at least once, and then swirl the background. Using a lighter and a darker wool allows you to highlight some areas of the rug, to sort of "spark up" the rug.

7. Hook a second wool into the border, for example, the wool you used for the logs. Complete the border by adding four rows of your border wool, making sure your corners are square (see page 45).

July Cabin Color Reference Guide

What a restful and safe feeling this peaceful scene conveys—
so simple, and yet a powerful story.

—Barb

Watching Over Ewe
Artwork by Carol Endres

Rug design by Barbara Carroll
Hooked by Annette Allessio

Pictorial themes, often biblically-inspired, abounded in

American folk art rugs. In Watching Over Ewe, adapted from the

artwork of Carol Endres, the lion and the lamb live peacefully in

perfect harmony, with the bluebird of happiness nestled in the treetop.

Barb's Color Tips

Refer to the photograph of the finished rug to guide your choice of wool colors.

The lion needs both a quiet wool and a more textured wool, plus a couple of uneven hairs at the end of his tail.

The wood in the tree is done in a nubby check, which adds interest and some ruggedness. For the leaves, using a large plaid wool with lots of blue and green and a little rust makes them all look the same, yet differentiated. The blue in the bird picks up the blue in the leaves.

The two trees in the background are a nice addition to the rug, but they are not significant. Don't make them stand out.

The sheep are done in two different tweeds, one darker than the other.

Using a reddish-cream (here, a herringbone) for the path provides a great color spark in that area of the rug and keeps the color flowing from the house. A perfect choice!

The light shade of camel is effective for the sky, and the deeper shade of camel works for the grass. Keep in mind that the sky doesn't have to be blue or the grass green.

The border has two rows of a neat plaid and three rows of the wool used in the house.

Learning the Basics

Before you begin, refer to Rug Hooking Basics, pages 22–51, a complete guide to selecting, dyeing and cutting the wool; transferring the design to the background; gathering materials and supplies; hooking the rug; and finishing and caring for your rug. You'll find materials for the rug motifs, background, border, and binding listed below.

For the lion
- 130 square inches (10" x 13") total

For the large tree
- 150 square inches (10" x 15")
- Several strips about 18" long for leaves
- Several strips for the bird

For the house
- Several strips in various colors

For the background trees
- 24 square inches (8" x 3")

For the sheep
- 132 square inches (10" x 14") total for bodies
- Several strips for the legs and faces
- Several strips of wool for the star

For the path
- 60 square inches (10" x 6")

For the ground
- 1/2 yard (6 ounces)

For the sky
- 3/4 yard (9 ounces)

For the border
- 2/3 yard (8 ounces) total

For the binding
- 10 feet of cotton binding tape, pre-washed
- 37 strands of 3-ply tapestry yarn

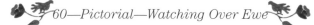

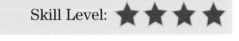

Hooking the Rug

Finished size: 26" x 26"
Size 8.5 cut

Skill Level: ★★★★

1. Begin with the lion. Cut some wool strips a little narrower, and use them to hook the features in his face. Keep his features very simple. Outline his face with a textured wool, and then fill in his face with a quiet wool. Outline and fill in the mane area. Using the same outlining wool, outline the rest of the lion and hook the definition lines for the legs. Give him a few uneven hairs at the end of his tail. Then fill in the lion's body with the softer wool.

Tip: Be careful not to crowd the lion's features. If they sort of "fall in," just take them out and rehook them. You can use the same wool strips.

2. Hook the tree trunk, following the shape of the tree, staying inside the lines. The leaves are mostly up, loop, up, and clip. Hook the bird on the treetop.

3. Hook the small house. The windows are up, loop, up, and clip. The door is up, loop, loop, up, and clip. Use the same wool for outlining and filling in the house, staying inside the lines of the house and being careful not to crowd the windows and door. Outline and fill the roof. The chimney is just up, loop, up, and clip, and then one row of grayish (or purplish?) wool for the smoke.

4. Hook the small trees, using the same wool for the trunks and foliage. Make sure you stay just inside the lines.

5. Hook the two sheep next. Hook the facial features, keeping them simple. Outline and fill the faces with the dark wool, being careful not to crowd the features. Use a lighter wool for the ears and a fun tweed for the bodies; you can make one darker than the other. Hook the legs in dark wool.

6. Go back up and hook the star, outlining and filling, keeping just inside the lines. Follow the shape of the star and make nice sharp points; directions for points are on page 42.

7. Hook the line between the border and the background. Use the same wool for the horizon line and the definition lines below the sheep.

8. Hook the path, and then hook the grass area and the sky area. For both areas, hook around all the motifs at least once and then fill them in. You do not need to hook in any particular direction; this gives the rug more of a folk-art feel.

9. Hook two rows of plaid in the border, and complete the border with three more rows, making sure your corners are sharp (see page 45).

Watching Over Ewe
Color Reference Guide

Maple Sugar Hearts

This treasure of a small rug is a heartwarming gift for your best friend.
Yes, I gave this rug to my great friend Bobbie True, who has a heart of gold.
—Barb

Maple Sugar Hearts
Artwork by Barbara Carroll

Rug designed and hooked by
Barbara Carroll

The antique maple sugar mold shown here was the
inspiration for Barb's *Maple Sugar Hearts* rug. As in many primitive
works of art, particularly Native American and Amish,
a single element of a repetitive theme is purposely "at odds,"
to convey that nothing in creation is perfect—only the Creator. In this
rug featuring a dozen hearts, one is a heart of gold!

Refer to the photograph of the finished rug to guide your choice of wool colors.

Using several shades of red, plus a red paisley, gives a nice variation to the hearts (see page 25).

One heart out of the dozen is hooked in gold because my head sort of goes to oddity in the rugs.

Mix your darks for the background; ten would not be too many.

Learning the Basics

Before you begin, refer to Rug Hooking Basics, pages 22–51, a complete guide to selecting, dyeing and cutting the wool; transferring the design to the background; gathering materials and supplies; hooking the rug; and finishing and caring for your rug. You'll find materials for the rug motifs, background, border, and binding listed below.

For the hearts
- 300 square inches (10" x 30") total red wools

For the background
- 300 square inches (10" x 30") total darks

For the border
- 260 square inches (10" x 26") of reds for 2 rows

- 260 square inches (10" x 26") of gold for 1 row

- 300 square inches (10" x 30") of black for 2 rows

For the binding
- 6 feet of cotton binding tape, pre-washed

- 25 strands of 3-ply tapestry yarn

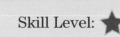

Hooking the Rug

Finished size: 25" x 10"
Size 8.5 cut

Skill Level: ⭐

1. Hook the hearts first, filling them with a random mix of reds.

Tip: Because the hearts are small, you might want to give them a nice crisp shape by outlining them with a background wool, hooking just outside the lines.

2. Hook the first row in the first border. This will contain the background as you hook it. If you have not already done so, outline the hearts with background wool. Outline the first row of the border with background wool, and then fill in the rest of the background.

3. Hook the remaining rows in the border. Make sure to keep the corners square (see page 45).

Maple Sugar Hearts
Color Reference Guide

Mollie's Star

A small square hooked rug works well as a
a table mat or as an inviting pillow top.
—Barb

Mollie's Star
Artwork by Barbara Carroll

Rug designed and hooked by
Barbara Carroll

Often a sampler rug incorporates many of the motifs
or geometric shapes a rug hooker needs to practice in mastering the
art of rug hooking. Here, *Mollie's Star*, designed by Barb and
affectionately named after Wayne's grandmother, provides a
star with points, circles, and border stripes for "practice makes perfect."

Refer to the photograph of the finished rug to guide your choice of wool colors.

For the star, use a wool that will give you a sharp outline so the star stands out against the background behind it. A red plaid is a good choice for the star, zigzag line, and fourth circle.

In the zigzag areas, pick up colors that are already in the rug. You could also hook it with leftover strips from other rugs, using whatever you have in your scrap basket.

A size 8.5 cut is recommended for most of the wool strips in this project, but use a size 10 cut for the red strips in the zigzag line. The wider size creates a stronger line.

Learning the Basics

Before you begin, refer to Rug Hooking Basics, pages 22–51, a complete guide to selecting, dyeing and cutting the wool; transferring the pattern to the background; gathering materials and supplies; hooking the rug; and finishing and caring for your rug. You'll find materials for the rug motifs, background, border, and binding listed below.

For the star, zigzag line, and fourth circle
- 300 square inches (10" x 30")

For the star outline, third circle, and border outside the zigzag line
- 1/6 yard (2 ounces)

For the background behind the star
- 100 square inches (10" x 10")

For the first and sixth circles and one line in the border
- 180 square inches (10" x 18")

For the second and seventh circles
- 100 square inches (10" x 10")

For the fifth circle
- 120 square inches (10" x 12")

For the corners in the circle area and one line in the border
- 150 square inches (10" x 15")
- Several strips for the outside row of the border

For the binding
- 7 feet of cotton binding tape, pre-washed
- 30 strands of 3-ply tapestry yarn

Hooking the Rug

Finished size: 20" x 20"
Size 8.5 and 10 cuts

 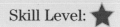

1. Start by outlining the star, staying just inside the line. Then fill the star, following its shape. Hook the first circle (the blue circle in the photograph). This will contain your hooking for the background around the star. Using the wool for the background around the star, hook one line around the star and one line on the inside of the first circle, and then fill the area.

Tip: You can fill in the background of the star either by echoing the shape of the star or by swirling the wool in funny directions. Either one is fun.

2. You can now hook the second, third, and fourth circles. Turn your frame as you hook, to make it easier.

3. Hook the line around the 14-inch square before you continue with the circles.

Technique tip: The remaining circles run into this line; you will need a "holding line" to contain your hooking.

4. Hook the remaining circles now, again turning your frame as you hook around them.

Mollie's Star Color Reference Guide

A Slice of Summer

This easy mix of melon and berries works up quickly and bands of coordinating color in the braided edge add the finishing touch.

—*Barb*

A Slice of Summer
Artwork by Warren Kimble

Rug design by Barbara Carroll
Hooked by Lynn Gabos

Fruit and berries were tantalizing treats for early settlers and were often themes of American folk art painting and rug hooking. Only four colors (black, white, green, and red) were used in Warren Kimble's *A Slice of Summer* for crisp, high-visual impact. The rug is complemented by bands of green and red in a braided border.

Refer to the photograph of the finished rug to guide your choice of wool colors.

For the rind, using a soft cream plaid that has a little sage green and red in it keeps the white part of the rind from being too white and drawing your eye to it.

A sparkly wool makes the leaves sort of shiny and fun. Using red for the veins in the leaves continues the play of red in the rug.

Use two reds for the strawberries to add interest.

For the inner border, try mixing three different plaids, one of them with some red to continue the color play in the rug.

Learning the Basics

Before you begin, refer to Rug Hooking Basics, pages 22–51, a complete guide to selecting, dyeing and cutting the wool; transferring the design to the background; gathering materials and supplies; hooking the rug; and finishing and caring for your rug. You'll find materials for the rug motifs, background, border, and binding listed below.

For the seeds, stems and leaf veins
- Small strips

For the watermelon rind
- 30 square inches of green (10" x 3")
- 90 square inches of white (10" x 9")

For the watermelon
- 220 square inches (10" x 22")

For the leaves
- 72 square inches (12" x 6")

For the strawberries
- 55 square inches (5" x 11") total reds

For the background
- 5/6 yard (10 ounces) total mixed dark wools

For the outer border
- 1/8 yard (1-1/2 ounces) green

For the inner border
- 1/4 yard (3 ounces) plaid

For an optional braided border
- 10 feet of 2-inch wide strips for each of the three strands

For the binding
- 7-1/2 feet of cotton binding tape, pre-washed
- 32 strands of 3-ply tapestry yarn

Hooking the Rug

Finished size: 14" x 29"
Size 8.5 cut

Skill Level:  ★ ★ ★

1. Hook the seeds in the watermelon first, just up, loop, up, and clip. Because the stem runs through part of the watermelon and is on top, hook the stem of the bottom right-hand leaf next, with just one row of the stem wool.

2. Hook the green rind, and then hook the white rind. Stay just inside the lines.

3. Outline the top of the red section of the watermelon, hook down along the white section, and then fill in the red, following the shape of the watermelon.

4. Hook the veins in the leaves (this is where you might want to use red). Hook the stem of the left-hand leaf. Outline and fill the leaves, making sure you stay just inside the line; do not crowd the veins.

5. Hook the green on the top of the strawberries, just one row of hooking. Then hook the strawberries.

6. Hook one row of the plaid wool between the background and the border. Cut all of the background wools, pile them together, and pull them randomly as you hook. Hook around everything once or twice, and then just swirl the wools as you fill in the background.

7. Hook an additional two rows of the plaid on the outer edge (making three rows). This keeps the play of color and gives a cheerful feel to the rug. Then hook two rows of green.

A Slice of Summer Color Reference Guide

Mister Hare

This is definitely a very stylized bunny, which makes for a fun rug to hook. The squares in the background are a great way to use any leftover strips of wool.

—*Barb*

Mister Hare
Artwork by Warren Kimble

Rug design by Barbara Carroll
Hooked by Chris Richey

Rabbits in the garden were a common, and often unwelcome, sight in early colonial days. However, when Barb spotted Mister Hare in Warren Kimble's portfolio of American folk art, she couldn't resist adapting the painting for rug hooking. The scattering of multi-color squares on the background adds contemporary flair to the folk art.

Refer to the photograph of the finished rug to guide your choice of wools.

A neat check works well for one of the "rabbit" wools, especially for outlining him.

For the border, consider a plaid that picks up the colors from the rabbit and some of the squares.

Think fun for the whiskers. Choose an unexpected wool for them.

Learning the Basics

Before you begin, refer to Rug Hooking Basics, pages 22-51, a complete guide to selecting, dyeing and cutting the wool; transferring the pattern to the background; gathering materials and supplies; hooking the rug; and finishing and caring for your rug. You'll find materials for the rug motifs, background, border, and binding listed below.

For the rabbit
- 1/6 yard (2 ounces) total wools
- Several strips for the bunny's eyes, nose, whiskers, and ears

For the background
- 1/6 yard (2 ounces) total
- Several strips of miscellaneous wools for the squares

For the border
- 1-1/4 yards (15 ounces)

For the binding
- 13 feet of cotton binding tape, pre-washed
- 35 strands of 3-ply tapestry yarn

Hooking the Rug

Finished size: 26" x 24"
Size 8.5 cut

 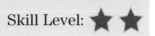

1. Hook the rabbit's facial features first. For the eyes, use the up, loop, up, and clip method; for the nose use up, loop, loop, up, and clip. For the whiskers, choose a fun wool and hook exactly on the lines.

2. Outline the rabbit (but do not outline the tail). This wool is also the rabbit's front feet. Fill in the ears with a soft wool. Fill in the rabbit, following the shape of his body. Also hook one row of your background wool around the bunny.

Tip: Outlining the rabbit at this point gives him a definite shape, but it also allows you to see the background color as you select wools for the squares.

3. Hook the squares next. Start with the outer square, hooking just on the line with your "outer" wool.

Hook the next area in with your "middle" wool, following the shape of the square. Then fill in the center, just up, loop, up, and clip.

4. Hook the line between the border and the background, hooking directly on the line. Using your background wool, hook at least one row around each of the squares as you did around the bunny, and one row next to the border line. Fill in the background in a sort of swirling pattern, or you can web the background; directions for these background techniques are on pages 44 and 45.

5. Now hook the border, making sure the corners are sharp; for making mitered corners see page 45.

Mister Hare Color Reference Guide

Two's Company

This is a delightfully simple rug with muted colors that are soothing to the eye. Notice how the background hooking echoes the shapes of the cows and the tree, and that the black spot on the right-hand cow is in the shape of the state of Vermont—Warren Kimble's home state. The rug can be finished with or without the braided border.

—*Barb*

Two's Company
Artwork by Warren Kimble

Rug design by Barbara Carroll
Hooked by Diane Denmead

The Holstein cows in Warren Kimble's Two's Company are widely-recognized motifs in his American folk art. First shown as Kissing Cows in an original painting, the reproduction prints and posters have sold millions of copies over the years. Typical of American folk art, the cows tower over a tree with bodies over-sized in comparison to their heads—but the overall look remains balanced.

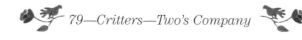

Refer to the photograph of the finished rug to guide your choice of wools.

The top of the tree was hooked with a teal, gold, and maroon check. This automatically gives shading and makes the tree more interesting. Trees don't have to be green.

The birds are hooked in a dark wool to balance the dark in the cows.

The hint of teal in the horizon line and grass lines comes from a windowpane plaid in medium taupe with teals.

The rug's dark border is hooked with several different blacks and a deep red.

Learning the Basics

Before you begin, refer to Rug Hooking Basics, pages 22-51, a complete guide to selecting, dyeing and cutting the wool; transferring the pattern to the background; gathering materials and supplies; hooking the rug; and finishing and caring for your rug. You'll find materials for the rug motifs, background, border, and binding listed below.

For the cows
- 1/4 yard (3 ounces) black
- 1/3 yard (4 ounces) white
- Several strips for the udders, ears, eyes, noses, horns, and hooves

For the tree
- 40 square inches (5" x 8")

For the birds
- Several strips

For the ground
- 1/2 yard (6 ounces) total

For the sky
- 1 yard (12 ounces) total

For the border
- 1/2 yard (6 ounces) total

For an optional braided border
- 15 feet of 2"-wide wool strips for each of the three strands of braiding

For the binding
- 11-1/2 feet of cotton binding tape, pre-washed
- 45 strands of 3-ply tapestry yarn

 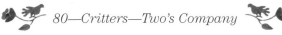

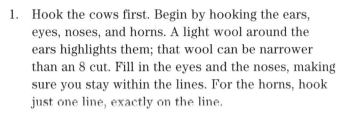

Hooking the Rug

Finished size: 20" x 46"
Size 8 cut

Skill Level: ★ ★ ★

1. Hook the cows first. Begin by hooking the ears, eyes, noses, and horns. A light wool around the ears highlights them; that wool can be narrower than an 8 cut. Fill in the eyes and the noses, making sure you stay within the lines. For the horns, hook just one line, exactly on the line.

2. Complete the cows' heads. Hook the white spots first, and then fill in the black area of the heads. Be very careful not to hook outside the lines.

3. Hook one line of your background wool around the two cows. (If you prefer, work on one cow at a time.) Hook this line just outside the line for the cows. Next hook in the black spots. Then outline the white area of the cows and fill it in, using the same white wool.

Tip: For a good-looking animal, hook the cows in the direction that the hair would be going on their bodies.

4. Hook the udder, hooking one line of a brighter pink for the outside and the teats, and filling in the rest with a quieter wool.

5. Hook the hooves with the same wool that you used for the black spots, hooking just one line across the bottom of each hoof.

6. Hook the tree, first the trunk and then the top, outlining and filling in the top of the tree by following the shape of the treetop.

7. Hook the birds, right on the line for each bird.

8. Hook the line between the background and the border. This contains your hooking and keeps the sides, top, and bottom nice and even.

9. Hook the line between the grass and sky area next. Then hook the grass lines with the same wool, hooking them in a sort of slope so they give the area some shape. Fill in the grass area with the wool chosen for the grass, hooking in the direction of the slope.

10. Hook the sky area, either by following the shape of the cows and the tree to echo those shapes, or by swirling the background and filling in the areas.

Tip: If you use a variety of wools, for example three different pale tones for the sky, cut them all and pile them all together. Then just pull random strips and hook them without worrying about which blue you should be using.

11. Hook two rows of hit-and-miss darks around the outside of the rug. If you choose to add the braided border, please refer to the braiding instructions on page 48.

Two's Company Color Reference Guide

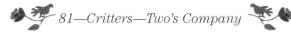

Debbie's Horse

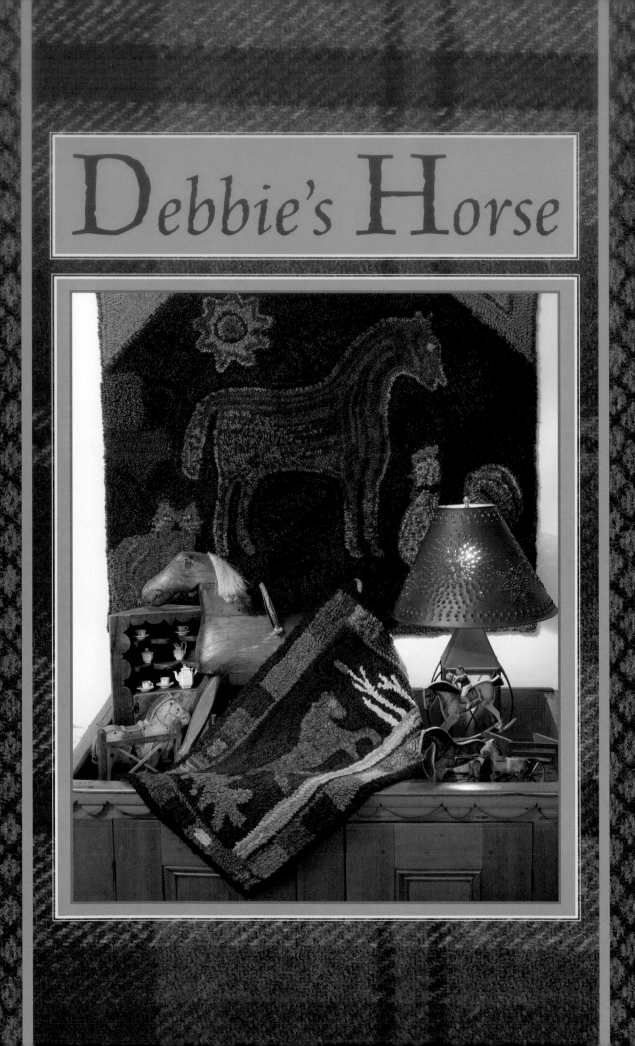

The center of this medium-sized rug is simple, and the border allows plenty of opportunity to play with color.

—Barb

Debbie's Horse
Adaptation of an antique rug

A Woolley Fox LLC rug pattern
Hooked by Barbara Carroll

Many of the antiques and collectibles and even the vintage rugs in Barb's collection are the inspiration for her new rug-hooking patterns. Debbie's Horse is a wonderful design from an antique rug, with its playful border of blocks of color that coordinate with the motif and background.

Refer to the photograph of the finished rug to guide your choice of wools.

Note that great paisley wools were used for the horse, trees, and cattail in this design (see page 25).

The squares in the border give you a chance to expand your use of wools. The spaces are not very big, and you will have a good time experimenting with different wools. Very exciting!

Remember that grass does not have to be green! Think fun!

Learning the Basics

Before you begin, refer to Rug Hooking Basics, pages 22-51, a complete guide to selecting, dyeing and cutting the wool; transferring the pattern to the background; gathering materials and supplies; hooking the rug; and finishing and caring for your rug. You'll find materials for the rug motifs, background, border, and binding listed below.

For the horse
- 240 square inches (60" x 4") total wools

For the tree
- 120 square inches (10" x 12")

For the cattails
- 60 square inches (10" x 6") total wools

For the grassy area
- 170 square inches (10" x 17")

For the background
- 1-1/3 yards (16 ounces) total wools

For the border
- 1/4 yard (3 ounces) total miscellaneous wools for squares

- 1/4 yard (3 ounces) for 2 rows of outer border

For the binding
- 8-1/2 feet of cotton binding tape, pre-washed

- 35 strands of 3-ply tapestry yarn

Hooking the Rug

Finished size: 18" x 30"
Size 10 cut

Skill Level: ★

1. Hook the eye of the horse first. (You can make it extra big, just for fun!) Outline the horse, staying just inside the lines, and then fill it in, following the shape of the horse. Hook the hooves, just up, loop, loop, up, and clip.

2. Hook the tree, again outlining just inside the lines and filling in the shape of the tree. Hook the cattails, hooking the cattail proper first and then the stem and branches.

Tip: Keep the cattails fairly slender, or you will lose the cattail effect.

3. Hook one line, exactly on the line between the border and the background, to contain your hooking of the background areas, and then hook the "grass" area.

4. Hook one line of background wool under the "grass" area. Use background to hook around each motif once, and then just swirl or web the background, following directions on pages 45 and 45.

5. The border is next. Hook two rows around the outside of the rug. Then comes the fun part! Just choose colors and wools that appeal to you, and maybe one or two wools that you are not sure of. Work around the rug in any direction; just pick where you want to start and keep going. As you come to the squares with small designs in them, hook the square first and then fill in around it.

Tip: Hook the border squares by hooking in the outside row first and continually turning your frame, hooking towards the center of the square.

Debbie's Horse Color Reference Guide

Laying Around

*The blue feathers on the chicken and the wire fencing in the
border absolutely make this rug. When hooking the feathers,
let your imagination run wild with the colors!*

—*Barb*

Laying Around
Artwork by Warren Kimble

Rug design by Barbara Carroll
Hooked by Nancy Tiernan

Friendly farm animals are a frequent theme in folk art
and Warren Kimble's chicken and chick are no exception.
Both are reminiscent of bygone days when chickens scratched for
food in the barnyard. The border replicates the chicken wire
that surrounded chickens in the coop—just *Laying Around*.

Barb's Color Tips

Refer to the photograph of the finished rug to guide your choice of wools.

Have fun with the comb and the wattle! They definitely do not need to be red; think purple, teal, green or a stripe. This makes your rug more interesting and fun.

You can hook each egg in a different wool, or hook two in one wool and the third in another. Maybe a hit-and-miss approach, using randomly selected "egg" colors, would be neat.

The warm light-rust wool for the wire fence in the border provides a nice warmth to the rug. Gray would have been too cool.

The line along the outside of the rug is done with a great blue and green plaid.

Learning the Basics

Before you begin, refer to Rug Hooking Basics, pages 22-51, a complete guide to selecting, dyeing and cutting the wool; transferring the pattern to the background; gathering materials and supplies; hooking the rug; and finishing and caring for your rug. You'll find materials for the rug motifs, background, border, and binding listed below.

For the chicken
- 100 square inches (10" x 10") of red
- 300 square inches (10" x 30") of blue
- 200 square inches (10" x 20") total wools for the feathers

For the chick
- 20 square inches (5" x 4") total of "wing" wool and "chick" wool
- Small strip for feet
- Small black strips for eyes

For the eggs
- 50 square inches (10" x 5")

For the grass
- 1/4 yard (3 ounces) total

For the sky
- 3/4 yard (9 ounces) total

For the border
- 2/3 yard (8 ounces)
- 120 square inches (10" x 12") for the wire line in the border

For the binding
- 10 feet of cotton binding tape, pre-washed
- 36 strands of 3-ply tapestry yarn

Hooking the Rug

Skill Level: ★ ★ ★

1. Hook the hen first. Begin with the eye, just up, loop, up, and clip. Fill the area around the eye, following the line. Hook the lines for the head feathers next, hooking directly on the lines. To fill in the head area, hook just inside the lines and follow the shape of the head feather area. Hook the comb and wattle next, again outlining just inside the lines and filling. Hook the beak.

2. Hook the feathers in the body. Use fun wools to outline and fill the areas. Remember to hook just inside the lines, and definitely use very playful wools. Hook the body next by outlining it and then filling it, hooking in the direction of the shape of the hen. Hook the tail feathers, outlining and filling.

Tip: Use the same wools that you used in the body feathers.

3. Hook the little chick now. Hook his eye—up, loop, up, and clip—and then hook his wing with the "wing" wool. Use the "chick" wool to outline and fill the body, making sure you do not crowd the eye and wing. Hook the beak next, and then the foot.

4. This rug does not have a separate line of color between the border and the backgrounds. Hook one line of the wool for the upper background around the inside of the border, down to the grass area. With a dark wool, hook a definition line between the border and the grass background, hook one line along the top of the grass area, and hook along the definition lines in the grass, just one row, exactly on the line.

5. Hook the eggs, outlining and filling. Then fill in the grass area; as you hook, follow the definition lines so that you have some slope in the grass.

6. Hook the upper background area next. Hook two rows around the hen, the chick, and the border area. Then have fun just sort of swirling the background wools.

7. Now hook the line on the outside of the rug. Hook the "wire fence" around the border. Fill in between the fence areas with your background wool.

Technique tip: By hooking the outside line first, you will be able to contain the fence wool and not end up with funny ends.

Laying Around Color Reference Guide

Meow Meow

This is a small, charming rug. Truly, in this case "less is more." The use of simple wools and color makes this rug a treasure. The only color in the rug is limited to the cats' faces and the outline around the cats. Great statement.

—Barb

Meow Meow
Artwork by Warren Kimble

Rug design by Barbara Carroll
Hooked by Cindy Dillow

Smiling white cats in the foreground were adapted for rug hooking from Warren Kimble's *Meow Meow* painting. In the background, the vintage rug with black cats (circa 1885) usually hangs above the four-poster bed in the master bedroom. For this photo it shares the stage with the cat duo for an afternoon of birdwatching!

Refer to the photograph of the finished rug to guide your choice of wools.

Each cat uses a different outlining wool, a soft camel and rust herringbone for the right-hand cat and a soft teal for the left-hand cat. Each cat is hooked in three different wools. Only the eyes are the same wool in both.

The wool used for the border is a simple but wonderful soft, black-and-beige plaid, which echoes the color play in the center of the rug.

The background contains several wools: A brown and black that ages the rug, a dark blue that highlights some areas, and a confetti wool that sparks up the background just a touch.

Think fun for the small face areas. They are fun to perk up, as with the pumpkin-orange whiskers on the right-hand cat.

Learning the Basics

Before you begin, refer to Rug Hooking Basics, pages 22-51, a complete guide to selecting, dyeing and cutting the wool; transferring the pattern to the background; gathering materials and supplies; hooking the rug; and finishing and caring for your rug. You'll find materials for the rug motifs, background, border, and binding listed below.

For the cats
- 1/2 yard (6 ounces) total of several wools
- Several strips for whiskers, eyes, and mouths

For the background
- 3/4 yard (9 ounces) total of several wools

For the border
- 200 square inches (10" x 20") of plaid wool

For the binding
- 8 feet of cotton binding tape, pre-washed
- 30 strands of 3-ply tapestry yarn

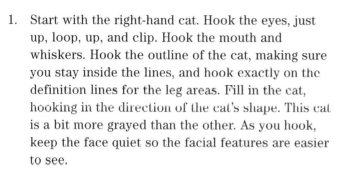

Hooking the Rug

Finished size: 18" x 25"
Size 8.5 and 9 cut

Skill Level:

1. Start with the right-hand cat. Hook the eyes, just up, loop, up, and clip. Hook the mouth and whiskers. Hook the outline of the cat, making sure you stay inside the lines, and hook exactly on the definition lines for the leg areas. Fill in the cat, hooking in the direction of the cat's shape. This cat is a bit more grayed than the other. As you hook, keep the face quiet so the facial features are easier to see.

Wool tip: This cat has three camel and taupe wools for its fur. Using these soft wools makes the rug look warm, cozy, and definitely loved.

2. Repeat these directions for the left-hand cat.

3. Hook the inmost row of the border wool next, to contain the hooking for the background. Then swirl the background; directions for backgrounds are on pages 44 and 45.

4. Hook the rest of the border, making sure to miter the corners as described on page 45.

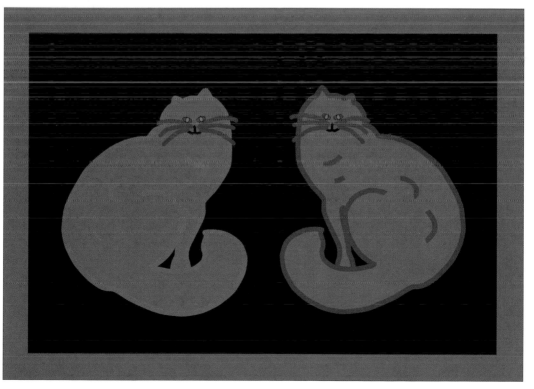

Meow Meow Color Reference Guide

Dappled Grey Horse

I love Warren Kimble's animals. They are wonderful, with a great sense of whimsy. The teal sky and blue-green grass make a terrific background for this nifty horse, and Warren's little clouds are wonderful.

—Barb

Dappled Grey Horse
Artwork by Warren Kimble

Rug design by Barbara Carroll
Hooked by Judy Wissler

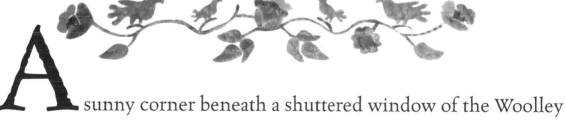

Asunny corner beneath a shuttered window of the Woolley Fox guest house is an ideal setting for showcasing Dappled Grey Horse, with a collection of Barb's antique horses and collectibles as the backdrop. Barb adapted the design for the hooked rug from original artwork by American folk artist Warren Kimble. The rug rests against an old newspaper delivery wagon topped by a vintage sprinkling can. The "farmhouse for the birds" was made by Ron Mazur.

Refer to the photograph of the finished rug to guide your choice of wools.

A beige and blackish-gray herringbone works well for the horse; a plaid is used for the mane and tail.

The first line between border and background is hooked in a blue and green plaid that moves softly around the rug.

The cloud is hooked in a very soft plaid, which gives nifty movement to the cloud.

The border contains colors picked up from the rest of the rug, tying the composition together.

Learning the Basics

Before you begin, refer to Rug Hooking Basics, pages 22-51, a complete guide to selecting, dyeing and cutting the wool; transferring the pattern to the background; gathering materials and supplies; hooking the rug; and finishing and caring for your rug. You'll find materials for the rug motifs, background, border, and binding listed below.

For the horse
- 1/4 yard (3 ounces) total wools
- Small strips for the house

For the trees
- 30 square inches (5" x 6") of orange wool(s)

For the grass
- 1/3 yard (4 ounces) total wools

For the cloud
- 30 square inches (5" x 6")

For the sky
- 5/6 yard (10 ounces)

For the border
- 5/6 yard (10 ounces) total wools

For the binding
- 10 feet of cotton binding tape, pre-washed
- 37 strands of 3-ply tapestry yarn

Hooking the Rug

Finished size: 25" x 28"
Size 8.5 cut

Skill Level: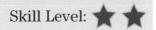

1. Hook the spots on the horse first. Begin on the outside of the spot, staying just inside the lines, and hook towards the center until the spot is filled in. Hook the eye and the nose next, again staying inside the lines so the features do not get too large.

2. Hook the mane and tail, outlining and filling with the plaid wool. Outline and fill in the horse's body, following the shape of the horse as much as you can.

3. Hook the trees. Five different oranges were used in this rug, one for each tree, but you can use all the same orange if you want. Because the trees are so small, use the same wool for trunk and tree.

4. The house is very small, so be patient with it. Start by hooking the windows, just up, loop, up, and clip. For the door, hook up, loop, loop, up, and clip. Hook the roof; horizontal hooking will be easier. Hook the chimney, using the up, loop, up, and clip method in a vertical line. Then hook the main part of the house.

Tip: Do not pack the wool into the house, and use a little narrower strip. Hooking the background will help stabilize the hooking in the house.

5. Hook the line between the border and the background, which will contain your hooking when you do the grass and sky. Next hook the line between grass and sky, and hook the grass lines. Fill in the grass area, either in no particular direction, or in the direction of the grass lines.

6. Hook the cloud, just outlining and filling. Outline the sky around all the various objects and along the border line. Fill the sky by using a swirling or lazy "S" motion; directions are on pages 44 and 45.

7. Hook the border with five rows of the wools used for the horse and its mane, a row of any orange, a row of grass green, and a row of deeper teal than is used in the sky.

Dappled Grey Horse Color Reference Guide

Flag Day Sheep

Just a fun patriotic rug, small—and who doesn't love the flag and a sheep!
—Barb

Flag Day Sheep
Artwork by Barbara Carroll

Woolley Fox LLC Design
Hooked by Barbara Carroll

Designed and hooked by Barb, *Flag Day Sheep* blends beautifully with her bucket of old flags and her extensive herd of collectible sheep of all shapes and sizes. This unusual folk art sheep designed by Diane Denmead boasts a mobile home— a miniature log cabin carried on his back.

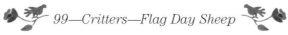

Refer to the photograph of the finished rug to guide your choice of wools.

In the canton of the flag, using a blue and white checked wool gives the impression of a blue field with white stars.

Try mixing two different light wools for the sheep's body.

The hooves are actually a darkish blue, more fun than black or gray.

The moon is a light blue and gray wool, to continue the color of the sheep. This helps keep the sheep from appearing too dominant in the rug.

The two stars are outlined with a red and camel herringbone wool. This creates warmth in the background; it also provides continuation of the red. The background is hooked in a darkish gold wool and a second wool that has a bit of spark to it.

The border is hooked in a great bouclé wool that has a lot of nubbiness to it.

Learning the Basics

Before you begin, refer to Rug Hooking Basics, pages 22-51, a complete guide to selecting, dyeing and cutting the wool; transferring the pattern to the background; gathering materials and supplies; hooking the rug; and finishing and caring for your rug. You'll find materials for the rug motifs, background, border, and binding listed below.

For the sheep
- 1/6 yard (2 ounces) total for the body
- Several small strips for the eye, nose, face, ears, legs, and hooves

For the flag
- 70 square inches (10" x 7") for the canton
- 75 square inches (5" x 15") for the red stripes
- 70 square inches (10" x 7") for the white stripes

For the background
- 5/8 yard (8 ounces) total wools

- Several small strips for the moon
- Several small strips to outline the stars

For the border
- Generous 3/8 yard (5 ounces)
- Several small strips for the line between border and background

For the binding
- 7-1/2 feet of cotton binding tape, pre-washed
- 30 strands of 3-ply tapestry yarn

Hooking the Rug

Finished size: 20" x 24"
Size 8.5 and 9 cuts, and size 10 cut for the border

Skill Level: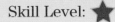

1. Begin by hooking the face of the sheep. For the eye, just hook up, loop, up, and clip in the blue wool, and then one row of gold around the blue. Outline and fill in the face, staying just inside the lines of the face. Hook the nose, again staying inside the lines, and then outline and fill in the ears, using a lighter wool for the area inside the right ear.

Technique tip: Outlining the ears keeps them clear against the sheep's body and the background.

2. Hook the flag next. Begin by outlining the left, right, and lower edges of the flag with the "sheep" wool. Hook the canton with blue and white check. Hook the stripes next, just hooking straight across horizontally. Some stripes might be wider than others; absolutely do not worry about that.

Tip: Outlining three edges of the flag gives the flag a sharper image, with well-defined lines.

3. Now hook the sheep's body. Start by outlining the sheep and the definition line between the two back legs. Fill in the sheep; mixing your wools, hook the side areas vertically and the area below the flag horizontally. Hook the legs in the same wool you used for the face, and hook the hooves.

4. Hook the moon. Make sure the points on the moon are sharp; directions for this are on page 42.

5. Hook one row right on the line between the border and background.

Technique tip: Stop hooking this line when you come to the moon, and then pick it up again on the other side of the curve of the moon. Do not hook the line around the top of the curve.

6. Hook the background. Outline the stars, keeping the points of each star sharp (see page 42).

Tip: The wider the cut, the more you see the textures in the wool. In Flag Day Sheep, the background wools are a size 9 cut to bring out their texture, and the nubby bouclé in the border is even more enhanced by a size 10 cut.

7. Hook the border, keeping your corners sharp.

Flag Day Sheep Color Reference Guide

Mister Scarecrow

This is a wonderful "harvest" rug. The swirling background looks as if the winds are whipping up to bring the apples and leaves down and winter will soon be on it's way. Don't you love the purple cat and bird?

—Barb

Mister Scarecrow
Artwork by Carol Endres

Rug design by Barbara Carroll
Hooked by Mary Cotter

Agenerously-sized *Mister Scarecrow* works up quickly with large expanses of swirling wool in muted colors for the background. Adapted for rug hooking by Barb from a Carol Endres original, it features many of the American folk trademark motifs. The hand-lettered HARVEST and the scarecrow are joined by a crow, a flag, a cat, and a stylized tree branch.

Refer to the photograph of the finished rug to guide your choice of wools.

The overalls are a blue herringbone with a windowpane of rust through it, and the shirt is a nifty plaid of green, red, blue, and gold. Use a fun color, maybe red, for the hat.

Hooking a bird in a tweed, small plaid, or check automatically makes the bird look "folky" in a primitive rug, with no shading necessary. Fun to do! The bird in this rug is hooked in a tweed of purple, teal, red, and gold, a wool that makes the bird come out looking like a crow.

The tree is hooked with a dark plaid and some striped wools, some duller and some brighter. The knot in the tree is a quiet tone.

The leaves are all hooked with the same orange, blue, and green check but with different colors used for the veins in the leaves. The apples each have several different reds, producing a great look.

To give the right look to the flag, use a blue check or a blue and white check for the canton and a red wool and a cream wool for the stripes.

For the baskets, try using a check for the bands and top of the baskets and a gold heather to fill in the baskets.

The rust wool in the letters continues the feel of "Fall in the air," and also carries the color from the leaves and the trim on the overalls.

And how about that purple cat!

Learning the Basics

Before you begin, refer to Rug Hooking Basics, pages 22-51, a complete guide to selecting, dyeing and cutting the wool; transferring the pattern to the background; gathering materials and supplies; hooking the rug; and finishing and caring for your rug. You'll find materials for the rug motifs, background, border, and binding listed below.

For the scarecrow
- 1/4 yard (3 ounces) of denim-blue for overalls
- 180 square inches (about 10" x 18") for outlining the overalls and for the letters
- Several strips for the patches
- 144 square inches (about 12" x 12") for the shirt
- 25 square inches (5" x 5") for the face
- Several narrower strips for facial features
- 45 square inches (9" x 5") for the hat
- Strip of plaid or check for the hatband
- 75 square inches (5" x 15") for the straw

For the bird and flag
- 75 square inches (5" x 15") for the bird
- 144 square inches (about 12" x 12") for the support and flagpole

- Several strips of red, white, and blue for the flag

For the apple baskets
- 144 square inches (about 12" x 12") total reds for the apples
- 35 square inches (7" x 5") total for baskets

For the tree
- 1/3 yard (4 ounces) total
- 144 square inches (about 12" x 12") total wools for the leaves

For the cat
- 35 square inches (7" x 5")

For the background
- 2-1/8 yards (26 ounces) total, in 3 different wools

For the border
- 2/3 yard (8 ounces) of darks

For the binding
- 13 feet of cotton binding tape, pre-washed
- 54 strands of 3-ply tapestry yarn

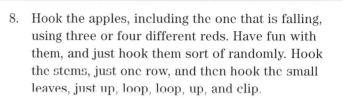

Hooking the Rug

Finished size: 45" x 31"
Size 8 cut

Skill Level: ★★★★

1. Hook the scarecrow's hatband. Outline the hat inside the lines, and fill it in. Hook the scarecrow's face with narrower strips, keeping features simple. Outline and fill the scarecrow's face with the "straw" wool without crowding the facial features.

2. Outline the overalls, straps and pockets using the rust herringbone. Hook the patches with fun wools. Hook the overalls with the denim-blue wool. Outline the shirt, staying just inside the lines, and fill it in. Hook the straw coming from the sleeves and pants legs, keeping it simple.

3. Hook the bird's eye, just up, loop, up, and clip. Hook his feet. Outline the bird, just inside the lines, and fill with the "bird" wool.

4. Hook the flag pole next, just one line, and then the flag, in the red, white, and blue "flag" wools.

Technique tip: To make the stripes start and stop evenly, first outline the flag with your background wool (staying just outside the lines) to contain the hooking.

5. Hook the baskets. Outline them with your background wool (staying just outside the lines). Use the checked wool on the bands and tops of the baskets, and the gold on the baskets themselves. Outline and fill the apples with a variety of reds, staying just inside the line. Do the stems next, just one line in a nice check or plaid. Hook the leaves with up, loop, loop, up, and clip.

6. Hook the cat. Use narrower strips for its features; use a bit of pink for the nose. Outline and fill, not crowding the features in the face and staying just inside the lines of the cat.

7. Outline and fill the tree next. Remember that its left edge is also the edge of the rug, so hook your last line very straight. For the leaves, hook the veins first, then outline and fill each leaf. Stay just inside the lines without crowd the veins.

Tip: If the veins "fall into" the leaves, just remove the wool out and hook it again.

8. Hook the apples, including the one that is falling, using three or four different reds. Have fun with them, and just hook them sort of randomly. Hook the stems, just one row, and then hook the small leaves, just up, loop, loop, up, and clip.

9. Using the wool that you plan to use for the right-hand and bottom borders, hook a row between those border areas and the background.

10. Cut all the background wools you plan to use, pile them, and randomly pull strips to use. Work in a swirling pattern (see pages 44 and 45).

Tip: Note the movement in the rug. It really looks as if the wind is swirling around. Some of this wonderful background echoes the shape of the motifs, some shows circular motion.

11. Hook the word HARVEST, hooking the letters very straight. Hook the background for the HARVEST border and for the bottom border. If the letters "fall in," rehook the letters, using the same strips. Note that there is no third-color line between the border and the background of this rug.

Keeping Watch

The eyes definitely have it here!
Just a wonderful autumn rug—easy to hook and easy to love.
—Barb

Keeping Watch
Artwork by Warren Kimble

Rug design by Barbara Carroll
Hooked by Caron Mazur

Wise old owl appears to be *Keeping Watch* as he listens intently to the animated chatter of jolly jack-o'-lantern. In this night scene, they share a fence in a Halloween-themed rug adapted from a Warren Kimble original.

Refer to the photograph of the finished rug to guide your choice of wools.

Keep the owl's eyes bright; they are the focal point of the owl.

Use several wools for the owl. Use a lighter tone for the definition lines within the large wing and a reddish tone for the definition line between the wing and the body, to make a clear difference. Make his talons a brightish gold.

A wonderful antique paisley was used for the star and another great paisley for the tree (see page 25).

The light and dark teal in the moon picks up the owl's eyes.

Try a soft orange plaid or heather wool for the jack-o'-lantern.

The wool for the fence needs to be a color strong enough to "carry" the owl and jack-o'-lantern, not too light and not plain brown. And a red fence is more fun anyway!

Learning the Basics

Before you begin, refer to Rug Hooking Basics, pages 22-51, a complete guide to selecting, dyeing and cutting the wool; transferring the pattern to the background; gathering materials and supplies; hooking the rug; and finishing and caring for your rug. You'll find materials for the rug motifs, background, border, and binding listed below.

For the owl
- 1/4 yard (3 ounces) total of several wools

For the jack-o'-lantern:
- 300 square inches (10" x 30") dark and light oranges
- Several strips of dark wool for the eyes, nose, and mouth, and for the bird
- Several strips of white for the eyes
- Strip of green for the stem

For the moon
- 75 square inches (5" x 15")

For the star
- 40 square inches

(10" x 4")

For the fence
- 360 square inches (60" x 6")

For the tree
- 300 square inches (10" x 30")

For the background
- 1 yard (12 ounces)

For the border
- 5/8 yard (8 ounces) total of mixed darks

For the binding
- 10 feet of cotton binding tape, pre-washed
- 37 strands of 3-ply tapestry yarn

Hooking the Rug

Finished size: 23" x 29"
Size 8.5 cut

Skill Level: ★ ★ ★

1. Begin with the owl's face. Staying just inside the lines, fill in the pupils and then hook the iris around the pupils. Hook the area around the eyes, staying inside the lines and following the shape. Hook the beak, with your loops going across but coming down in a straight line. Outline the rest of the head, and fill in the area that remains.

2. Hook the large wing next. Use a lightish wool to hook the definition lines in the wing, and then use your "wing" wool to outline the wing and fill it in following the shape of the wing. Hook a contrasting definition line just next to the wing.

3. Outline the left side of the body and the legs, and use the same wool to hook the definition line down the middle of the body. Fill in the owl's body, hooking horizontally and using several different wools to give the effect of the "feather lines." Fill in the legs. With a gold wool, outline and hook the talons, and then hook the tail feathers, following the shape of the feathers and staying just inside the lines. (Isn't he a great bird?)

4. Hook the jack-o'-lantern next, beginning with his eyes. Outline the eye area with a deeper orange, and then fill it in, white wool to the left and dark wool to the right. Use the same dark wool to outline and fill the nose. Outline the mouth with the same wool that you used to outline the eyes, and fill it in with the same dark you used for the eyes and nose.

5. Use the deeper orange wool to outline the whole jack-o'-lantern and to hook the definition lines. Fill in the jack-o'-lantern with the softer orange. Hook the stem, and then hook the bird. Again, stay in the lines.

6. Hook the star, outlining and filling, following the shape of the star. Keep the points nice and sharp; there are directions for this on page 42.

7. Hook the line between the border and the background. Using orange keeps the spirit of autumn and moves the pumpkin color around the rug.

8. Hook the bare tree. Again, think about color, not just a plain brown. Notice how great the paisley works here.

9. Do the fence next, first hooking the definition lines in a darker shade and then filling in with your "fence" wool. Hook the uprights vertically and the back rail horizontally.

10. Outline the moon now, and then hook in the lighter teal for the face, staying just on the lines. Go back to the darker teal and fill in the rest of the moon, being careful not to crowd the face.

11. Finally, hook the background. Outline all the motifs at least once, and then swirl the background or hook in a lazy "S" manner. Directions for this technique are on pages 44 and 45.

12. Hook the border in "hit or miss" fashion to pick up the wools in the owl. Cut all your darks, pile them together, and randomly pull out strips for hooking.

Keeping Watch Color Reference Guide

Frosty Friends

This joyful tribute to winter is sure to make anyone smile. The rug is an invitation to play with the wools and not be too serious.

—*Barb*

Frosty Friends
Artwork by Carol Endres

Rug design by Barbara Carroll
Hooked by Lisa Baughman

Folk art pictorials often provide the artist an opportunity to incorporate many unrelated motifs around a central theme. In the hooked rug *Frosty Friends*, adapted from artwork by Carol Endres, cats, flowers, fences, houses, snowmen, and even an outhouse topped by a larger-than-life cardinal take center stage in this heartwarming winter scene. Sharing the fun are Bobbie's Snow Lady Doorstop and Barb's Frosty Doorstop, cozying up to the popped corn and hot chocolate by the fireplace in the Woolley Fox guesthouse.

Barb's Color Tips

Refer to the photograph of the finished rug to guide your choice of wools.

Using a soft plaid for the windows gives a nice glow and is more interesting than using a wool with very little pattern to it.

A very soft plaid of green and taupe with a bit of red makes the roof look a little snowy.

The chimney wool—a maroon and taupe small plaid—gives the effect of brick and mortar; big fun!

To make the path look like gravel, try a black, gray, and off-white small tweed.

The snowmen are hooked with a brighter white for contrast.

For the effect of snow on the evergreen branches try a green and white herringbone.

Wintertime trees don't need to be brown and gray. Hook them in a small plaid or check or herringbone, not too dark so the branches stand out against the sky; this rug uses a soft gray, blue, and red small check.

Just for fun, the cat is green—doesn't everyone have a green cat? Or choose your own "kitty color."

Using a red and cream herringbone wool for the fence makes a light and fun contrast with the snow. It also moves the red around the rug.

For contrast with the dark sky, use a sparkly wool for the birdhouse.

Learning the Basics

Before you begin, refer to Rug Hooking Basics, pages 22-51, a complete guide to selecting, dyeing and cutting the wool; transferring the pattern to the background; gathering materials and supplies; hooking the rug; and finishing and caring for your rug. You'll find materials for the rug motifs, background, border, and binding listed below.

For the house and outhouse
- 1-1/3 yards (16 ounces) total of reds
- Several strips for doors, window frames, and windows
- 150 square inches (10" x 15") for the house roof
- 60 square inches (10" x 6") for the outhouse roof

For the path
- 50 square inches (10" x 5")

For the evergreen tree and other branches
- 60 square inches (10" x 6")

For the snowman with the striped sweater
- 75 square inches (5" x 15") total of all wools

For the snowman with the red coat
- 100 square inches (10" x 10") total of all wools

- Several strips of wool for the cat
- Several strips of wool for winter trees

For the fence
- 1/8 yard (2 ounces)

For the stars
- 30 square inches (5" x 6")

For the birdhouse
- 75 square inches (5" x 15") total wools

For the red birds
- 45 square inches (5" x 9")

For the snow on the ground
- 1-1/4 yards (15 ounces)

For the sky
- 1-1/2 yards (18 ounces)

For the border
- Generous 3/4 yard (10 ounces)

For the binding
- 14 feet of cotton binding tape, pre-washed
- 55 strands of 3-ply tapestry yarn

Hooking the Rug

Finished size: 24" x 55"
Size 8 cut

Skill Level: ★ ★ ★ ★

1. For the front door, use red to hook one row for the bow and two rows for the wreath and to outline the door and the windows. Fill in the door, hooking vertically. Outline the windows, hook the crossbars, and fill in the windows, hooking vertically.

2. Hook two rows with green for the house roof lines; outline and fill hooking horizontally. Hook the chimney; outline and fill the house.

3. Outline and fill the outhouse roof, star, following its shape and making sharp star points. Outline the door, using one row. Outline and fill the quarter-moon, and then fill in the door with vertical rows. Hook the windows vertically. Outline and fill in the outhouse, using the same wool, hooking vertically.

4. Hook the candy canes using a bright red and white. Hook the "gravel" path, following its lines.

5. For the red cardinals, make the eyes black, just up, loop, up, and clip. Hook the beaks with a sharp point, and one row for the feet. Outline and fill.

6. For the snowman with striped sweater, use odd shades of darks to hook his eyes, mouth, and buttons. Use a fun wool for the scarf. Hook the face with snowman wool; add a bright hat. Use narrower strips of wool for the scarf fringe. Outline the sweater with "snow" wool outside the line. Hook the stripes and the body in the shape of a ball. Hook the twig "hands," using one row of hooking.

7. For the other snowman, hook the eyes, nose, and mouth with various darks. Hook the line down the jacket, and the buttons. Use a fun plaid for the scarf, with narrower wool for the fringe. Hook the face and add a jaunty hat. Outline and fill the jacket. Hook the body, finish with the arms.

8. Use the green and white wool for the evergreen trunk and branches, the greenery, the branches in the pots, and the bush. Hook just one row for all branches and stems. Use your soft small check or plaid to hook one row for the winter trees.

9. Outline, and fill the cat. For the eyes, hook up, up, and clip. Use a strip of narrower wool for whiskers.

10. Hook the pot and the candle, hooking horizontally. Top the candle with an orange or gold flame.

11. Outline and fill the birdhouse roof with a neat plaid. Hook the little hole, just up, loop, up, and clip. Outline and fill the house with red. Hook the post; sparkly wool shows up nicely against the sky.

12. Hook the fence with red and cream wool. Outline and fill the stars, making sharp points.

13. With border wool, hook the line between border, snow and sky. With a darker "snow wool," hook snow lines under the bush, snowman, and birdhouse. Hook snow line between snow and sky with a rolling motion. Hook the sky, letting the wool give movement. Hook the border, squaring the corners.

 113—Winter Holiday—Frosty Friends

Bobbie's Snow Lady Doorstop

This is a fun friend for the Frosty doorstop. Note the 'confetti' wool that the body is hooked in. Lots of fun!
—Barb

Designed by Barbara Carroll
Hooked by Bobbie True

Barb's Color Tips

Refer to the photograph of the finished rug to guide your choice of wools.

For the "snow" wool, use just one wool, such as a soft plaid, or you can use several nice textured off-whites.

Learning the Basics

Before you begin, refer to Rug Hooking Basics, pages 22-51, a complete guide to selecting, dyeing and cutting the wool; transferring the pattern to the background; gathering materials and supplies; hooking the rug; and finishing and caring for your rug. You'll find materials for the rug motifs, background, border, and binding listed below.

- 2/3 yard (8 ounces) of "snow" wool
- 100 square inches (10" x 10") for the hat
- Small strips for buttons, nose, mouth, and eyes
- 7" x 7" square of plaid, tweed, or check for the shawl
- Yarn that matches the wool
- Needle with a large eye
- 8" x 8" piece of fabric for the bottom of the doorstop
- Aquarium rock
- Craft polyfil
- Twigs for arms
- Mechanical cutter, or rotary cutter and mat
- Red Dot Tracer™ or nylon organdy
- Black fine-point Sharpie marker
- Fray-Chek™

1. Machine-stitch all around the Snow Lady patterns, about 1/2" outside the line. Apply Fray-Chek around the patterns, on the edge of the machine stitching; this helps ensure that the backing will not pull apart when it is trimmed after hooking.

2. Hook the front of the Snow Lady. Outline and fill the hat, using a fun plaid or check. Hook the eyes, using the up, loop, up, and clip method. Outline and fill the red heart for the nose. Hook just one line of a dark wool for the mouth. Hook the buttons, outlining them and filling them in, each in its own color. Hook the rest of the front, outlining and then filling, following the lines of the body. As you hook the face, be careful not to hook too close to the eyes, nose, and mouth.

3. Hook the back of the Snow Lady just as you did the front but without eyes, nose, mouth, and buttons.

4. After the Snow Lady is hooked, press both pieces. Lay the piece, right side facing down, on the ironing board. Place a damp

Hooking the Doorstop

Finished size: 12" high
Size 8 cut

towel on the backing. With a hot iron, press the entire hooked area; do not iron it. Turn the hooking right-side up, place the damp towel on it, and again press it. Allow both pieces to dry thoroughly.

5. Trim 3/4" around the Snow Lady, front and back. Using a needle with a large eye and a yarn that closely matches the color of the wool, whipstitch the two pieces together, right sides out, tucking the trimmed backing inside.

Important: You must leave holes for the Snow Lady's twig "arms." To do this, decide where you want the arms to be and, on the backing, make two marks about 3/4" apart, to indicate the armhole. With the two pieces laid together, start on one side at the lower armhole mark and whipstitch only one edge of the armhole (tucking in the backing) for 3/4", to the upper armhole mark. Then begin joining the front to the back, whipstitching all around the head. Continue down to the upper mark for the other armhole. Whipstitch only one side for 3/4" (tucking in the backing), and tie off the yarn. To join the rest of the front to the back for that side, start from the bottom, whip up to the armhole, and whip the one edge for the armhole that has not been done. Go back to the other side; again, start from the bottom, whip up to the armhole, and whip the one edge for the armhole that has not been done.

6. Fill the hat, head, and middle with craft polyfil. Sew a round piece of fabric on the bottom, leaving an opening. Fill the bottom with aquarium rock, and sew around the bottom until it is closed.

Tip: Do not use beans, rice, or any other foodstuff to weight a doorstop. The "critters" find a nice new home with plenty to eat, and they move right in!

7. For the shawl, fold a 7" x 7" square of wool in half diagonally to get a triangle 10" wide and 5" tall. No need to hem it—just wrap it around the Snow Lady's shoulders and tie the ends.

8. Add arms, using interesting twigs from a tree or bush.

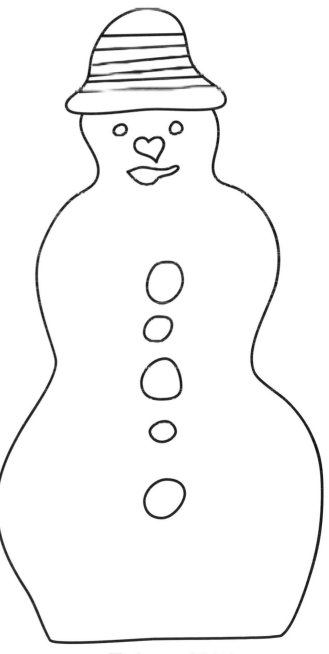

Enlarge 200%

Barb's Frosty Doorstop

This is a fun project, easy to do and a smile to work on. Finding old buttons for the snowman is neat, but remember that the buttons do not all need to match!

—Barb

Designed and hooked by Barbara Carroll

Barb's Color Tips

Refer to the photograph of the finished snowman to guide your choice of wools.

Frosty can be hooked with one wool, such as a soft plaid, or you can use several nice textured off-whites.

Use dark navies, greens, or purples for the eyes and mouth. These colors give you a softer dark, and they make a smooth color transition.

Learning the Basics

Before you begin, refer to Rug Hooking Basics, pages 22-51, a complete guide to selecting, dyeing and cutting the wool; transferring the pattern to the background; gathering materials and supplies; hooking the rug; and finishing and caring for your rug. You'll find materials for the rug motifs, background, border, and binding listed below.

- 2/3 yard (8 ounces) of "snow" wool
- Several strips for facial features
- 200 square inches (10" x 20") for the hat
- Scrap of wool fabric for a scarf, about 1-1/4" x 21"
- Interesting buttons
- Yarn that matches the wool
- Needle with a large eye
- 8" x 8" piece of fabric for the bottom of the doorstop
- Aquarium rock
- Craft polyfil
- Twigs for arms

1. Machine-stitch all around the Frosty patterns, about 1/2" outside the line. Apply Fray-Chek around the patterns, on the edge of the machine stitching; this helps ensure that the backing will not pull apart when it is trimmed after hooking.

2. Begin with the hat, hooking in stripes or in a fun check or plaid wool. Outline the hat, and then hook the tassel. Then, just hook across the hat area if you are hooking stripes, or hook along the shape of the hat if you are using a check or plaid.

3. Hook in the eyes and mouth in one of the softer darks. To hook the nose, start on the widest area, come to a point, and then as you come back, sort of "cheat" to bring the wool back to where you can hook the second row under the first row.

4. Hook Frosty next, outlining and then filling, following the lines of the body. As you hook the face, be careful not to hook too close to the eyes, nose, and mouth.

5. Hook the back of Frosty just as you did the front but without eyes, nose, and mouth.

6. After Frosty is hooked, press both pieces. Lay the piece, right side facing down, on the ironing board. Place a damp towel on the backing. With a hot iron, press the entire hooked area; do not iron it. Turn the hooking right-side up, place the damp

Finished size: 14" high
Size 8 cut

Skill Level: ⭐

towel on it, and again press it. Allow both pieces to dry thoroughly.

7   Trim 3/4" around Frosty, front and back. Position the buttons on the front and sew them in place. Using a needle with a large eye and a yarn that closely matches the color of the wool, whipstitch the two pieces together, right sides out, tucking the trimmed backing inside.

Important: You must leave holes for Frosty's twig "arms." To do this, decide where you want the arms to be and, on the backing, make two marks about 3/4" apart, to indicate the armhole. With the two pieces laid together, start on one side at the lower armhole mark and whipstitch only one edge of the armhole (tucking in the backing) for 3/4", to the upper armhole mark. Then begin joining the front to the back, whipstitching all around the head. Continue down to the upper mark for the other armhole. Whipstitch only one side for 3/4" (tucking in the backing), and tie off the yarn. To join the rest of the front to the back for that side, start from the bottom, whip up to the armhole, and whip the one edge of the armhole that has not been done. Go back to the other side, and again start from the bottom, whip up to the armhole, and whip one edge for the armhole that has not been done.

8.   Fill the hat, head, and middle with craft polyfil. Sew a round piece of fabric on the bottom, leaving an opening. Fill the bottom with aquarium rock, and sew around the bottom until it is closed.

Tip: Do not use beans, rice, or any other foodstuff to weight a doorstop. The "critters" find a nice new home with plenty to eat, and they move right in!

9.   Add arms, using interesting twigs from a tree or bush. Tie the scarf around Frosty's neck, and he's ready to go to work.

Enlarge 200%

Eight Is Enough

For a festive holiday runner, give the lead reindeer a red nose.
After all, 'Tis the season!

—Barb

Eight Is Enough
Artwork by Carol Endres

Rug design by Barbara Carroll
Hooked by Penny Gessner

Which reindeer stayed home so Rudolph could play?
Who knows! Regardless, for this enchanting night-before-Christmas Santa,
sleigh and reindeer scene adapted for rug hooking from original artwork
by Carol Endres, *Eight Is Enough.*

Refer to the photograph of the finished rug to guide your choice of wools.

Two browns are used in each deer. Red is used for the reins to keep a spark of red going throughout the rug, ending at the lead reindeer's red nose.

Hooking the stars with a check or plaid makes them all look similar but with slight differences. Making one star different adds interest.

For the rows between border and background, try for a plaid that has colors similar to those in the rug.

You could use a mix of several darks, hooked randomly, for the background.

The border uses a deeper and brighter blue than the background, to make the rug richer.

Learning the Basics

Before you begin, refer to Rug Hooking Basics, pages 22-51, a complete guide to selecting, dyeing and cutting the wool; transferring the pattern to the background; gathering materials and supplies; hooking the rug; and finishing and caring for your rug. You'll find materials for the rug motifs, background, border, and binding listed below.

For the Santa
- 110 square inches (10" x 11") total of reds for coat, hat, and reins
- 20 square inches (5" x 4") for Santa's bag
- Several strips for the face
- Several strips of white for beard and fur
- Several strips for mitten and boot

For the sleigh
- 75 square inches (5" x 15")
- Several strips for outline and runners

For the reindeer
- 1/4 yard (3 ounces) for bodies
- 40 square inches (5" x 8") for horns

- Several varied strips for hooves
- Small strips for bells

For the stars
- 110 square inches (10" x 11") total

For the background
- 1-7/8 yards (21 ounces)

For the border
- 1/4 yard (3 ounces) for two-row stripe
- 3/8 yard (5 ounces) for outer border

For the binding
- 14 feet of cotton binding tape, pre-washed
- 57 strands of 3-ply tapestry yarn

Hooking the Rug

Finished size: 12" x 18"
Size 8 cut

Skill Level: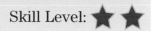

1. Begin with Santa's face. For the eye, hook up, up, and clip. Hook the fur on the hat, just one line, and hook the hat, outlining inside the lines and filling. Use the same wool for the hair and beard, as they run into each other and are so small that the eye will not pick up a difference between them. Fill in Santa's face, staying in the lines and being careful not to pack the wool in the face.

2. Hook the outline of the sleigh on the top and two sides of the sleigh, using the outline wool. Now, using the sleigh wool, outline across the bottom of the sleigh. Fill in the sleigh, hooking in the direction of its shape. Outline Santa's bag, just inside the line, and then fill it in with the same wool.

3. You are now ready to hook Santa's coat, fur, boot, and mitten. Begin with the coat, hooking a line for the belt and then filling in the coat within the coat lines and up against the lines for the sleigh and beard. Hook the fur and the bottom of the coat. Hook the boot. Outline and fill the mitten.

4. Hook the runners of the sleigh; this will be only one line of hooking.

Technical tip: Through the hooking so far, you have progressively contained all your hooking because of the order in which you have hooked these images. Always think about how to contain your hooking so that the image does not have uneven or odd shapes.

5. Hook the red reins, running from deer to deer. Hook the bells with the up, loop, up, and clip method, using a bright gold wool so the bells will be easily seen. Hook the eyes with the same up, loop, up, and clip.

6. Outline each deer and fill it in with the brown wools. Add the noses with up, loop, up, and clip. (Make the lead reindeer's nose red.) Hook the hooves, just one row across the bottom of each leg. The antlers on the eight reindeer are each hooked with a different wool, to add a bit of interest to the rug.

7. Hook the stars with a check or plaid. Make one of them different from the rest, to add interest. Be sure you hook the stars with nice sharp points; directions for doing so are found on page 42. Fill the stars by hooking in the direction of the star's shape.

8. Hook a double row of an interesting plaid between the border and the background. Hook the background next, hooking once around each of the motifs and along the double row and then fill the background. Swirl the background, or maybe try a lazy "S"; directions for these techniques are on page 00.

9. Hook the border area. Make sure that you miter the corners; you can find directions on page 42.

Eight Is Enough Color Reference Guide

Rug Hooking Resources

July Cabin, 25" x 47": one square equals one inch
Enlarge 600%

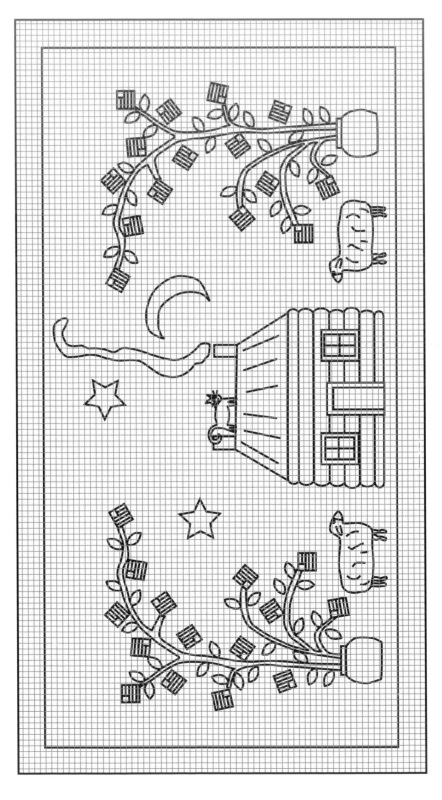

Watching Over Ewe, 26" x 26": one square equals one inch

Enlarge 400%

Maple Sugar Hearts, 25" x 10": one square equals one inch

Enlarge 300%

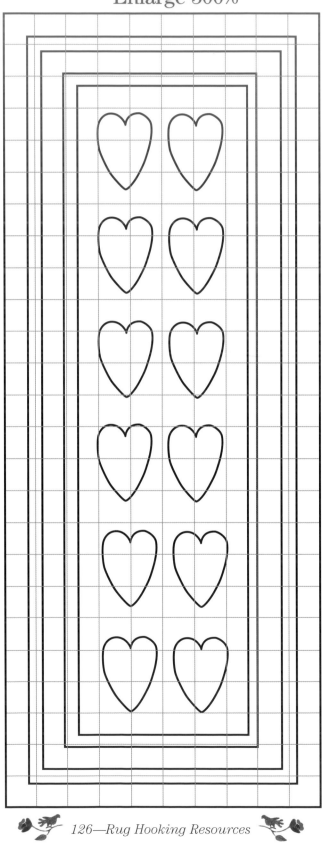

Mollie's Star, 20" x 20": one square equals one inch
Enlarge 300%

The Patterns

A Slice of Summer, 14" x 29": one square equals one inch

Enlarge 350%

Mister Hare, 20" x 24": one square equals one inch

Enlarge 275%

Two's Company, 20" x 46": one square equals one inch

Enlarge 600%

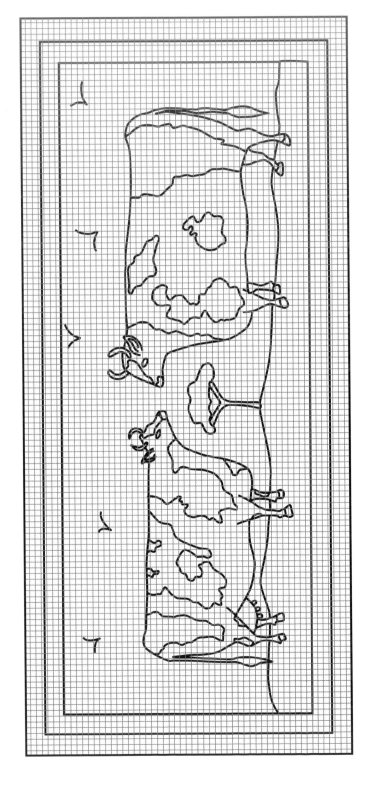

Debbie's Horse, 18" x 30": one square equals one inch
Enlarge 370%

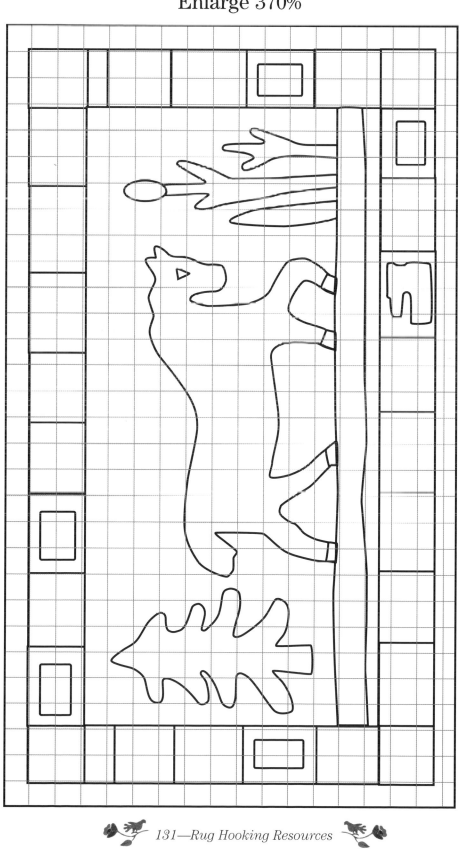

Laying Around, 21" x 30": one square equals one inch

Enlarge 370%

Meow Mcow, 18" x 25": one square equals one inch
Enlarge 327%

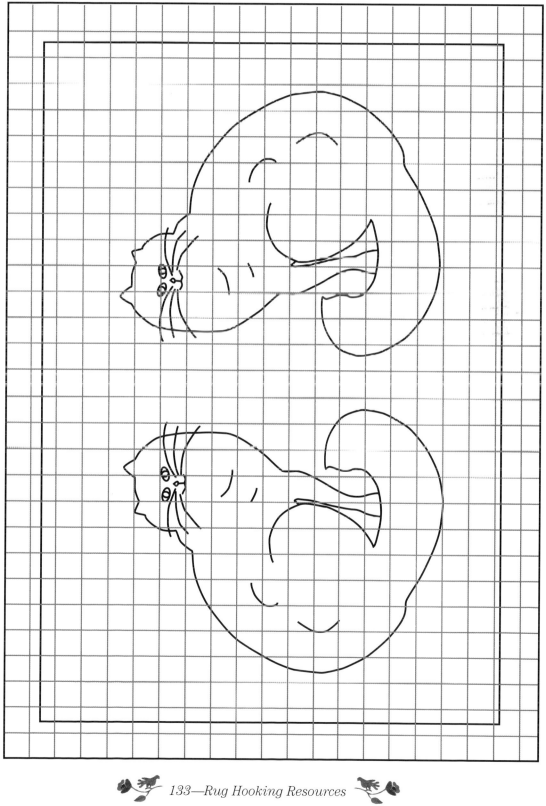

The Patterns

Dappled Grey Horse, 25" x 28": one square equals one inch

Enlarge 415%

Flag Day Sheep, 20" x 24": one square equals one inch
Enlarge 330%

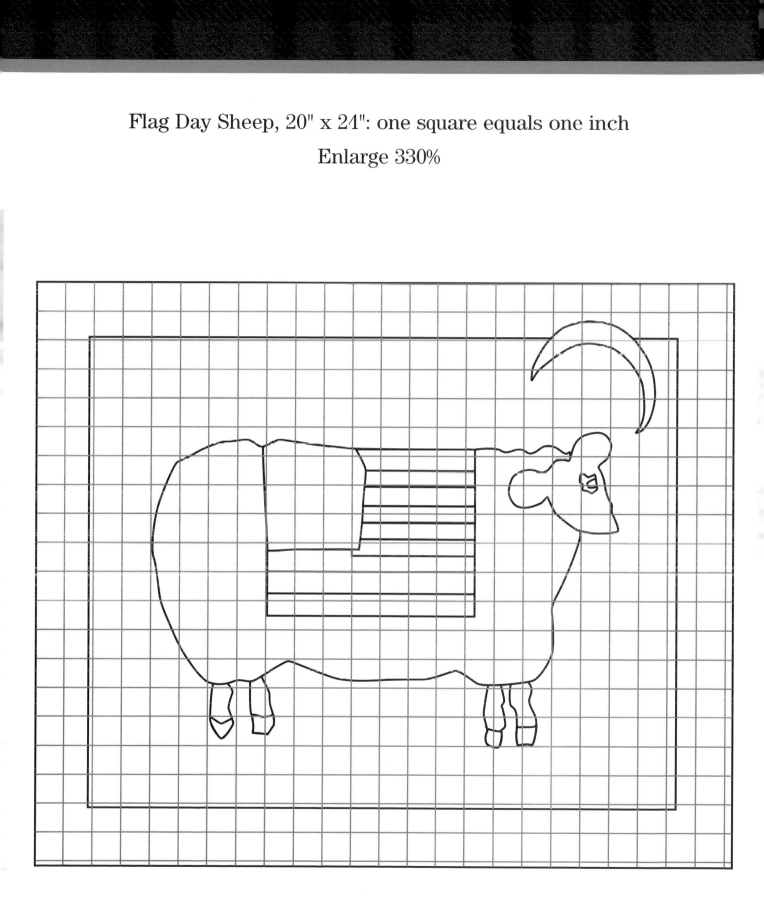

Mister Scarecrow, 45" x 31": one square equals one inch

Enlarge 515%

Keeping Watch, 23" x 29": one square cquals onc inch

Enlarge 370%

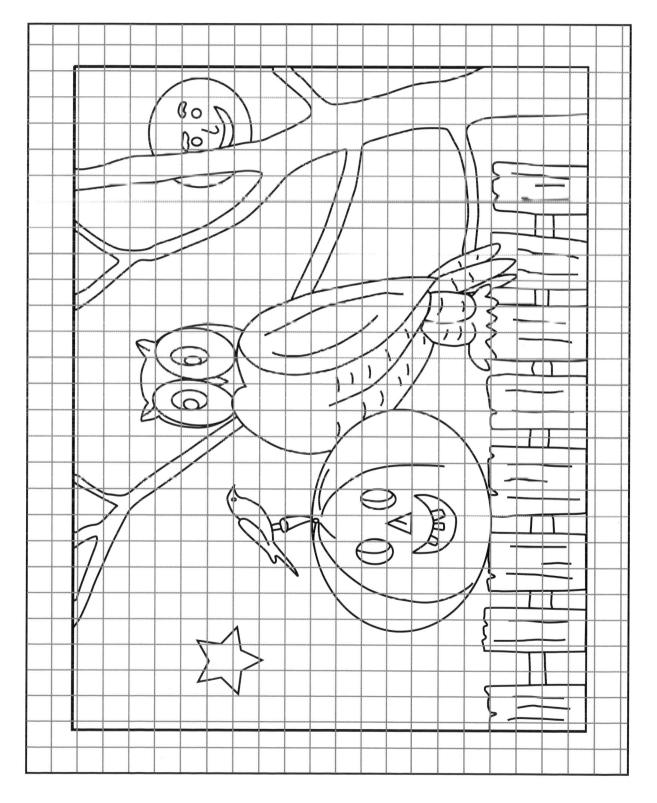

Frosty Friends, 24" x 55": one square equals one inch

Enlarge 685%

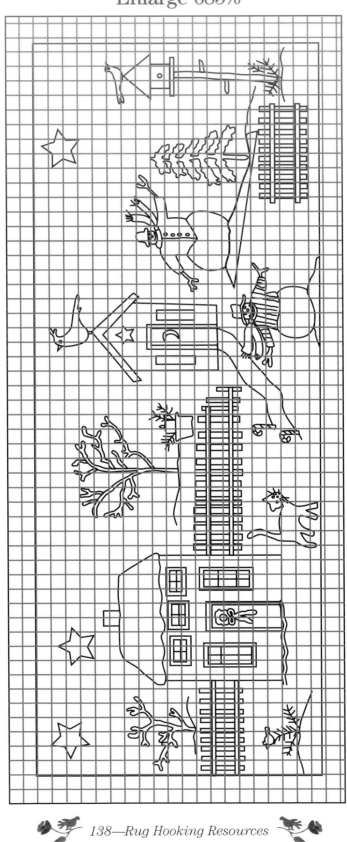

Eight Is Enough, 12" x 68": one square equals one inch

Enlarge 835%

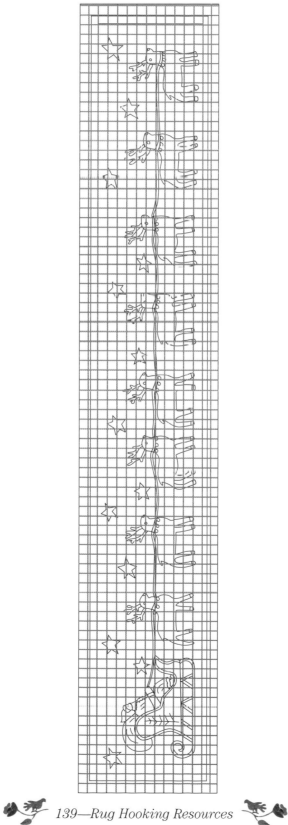

Nestled above the rocky Loyalhanna Creek, Ligonier, Pennsylvania, dates back to 1817 when it was a stagecoach stop between Philadephia and Pittsburgh. Horses rested in what is today The Diamond (above) Ligonier's trademark village square with its historic buildings and bandstand. A little farther east, the Compass Inn (below right) also offered travelers shelter. Fort Ligonier (below left) was built by the British as a place of military refuge during the French and Indian Wars.

About the Author

High school sweethearts, Wayne and Barbara Carroll have shared everything from prom to being proud grandparents. In retirement they still enjoy each other's company—working at the Woolley Fox. Barb teaches classes and Wayne handles the business. The Woolley Fox offers wool, supplies, and patterns printed by Pat and Paul Moshimer, through a catalog and retail stores. For more information about the Woolley Fox or to order a catalog, call 724-238-3600.

For Further Reference

Associations & magazines

ATHA (Association of Traditional Hooking Artists)
Joan Cahill, Membership Chairman
600 Maple Street
Endicott, NY 13760
607-748-7588
jcahilll29@aol.com
www.atharugs.org

Rug Hooking Magazine
1300 Market Street, Suite 202
Leymoyne, PA 17043-1420
800-233-9055
rughook@paonline.com
www.rughookingonline.com

The Wool Street Journal
312 North Custer
Colorado Springs, CO 80903
888-784-5667
www.woolstreetjournal.com

Books

American Primitive Hooked Rugs by
Barbara Carroll and Emma Lou Lais

Antique Colours for Primitive Rugs by
Emma Lou Lais and Barbara Carroll

The Secrets of Primitive Hooked Rugs by
Barbara Carroll with Susan Huxley

Rugs for My Red Cape by
Edyth O'Neill
4611 West Highway 290
Fredericksburg, TX 78624
eoneilli@ktc.com

Warren Kimble, American Folk Artist by
Warren Kimble
Landauer Corporation
131 NW 101st Street, Suite A
Urbandale, IA 50322
800-557-2144
www.landauercorp.com

Cutters

Harry M Fraser Company
433 Duggins Road
Stoneville, NC 27048
336-573-9830
fraserrugs@aol.com
www.fraserrugs.com

Townsend Industries Inc.
Box 97
Altoona, IA 50009
877-868-3544
t51info@t-51.com
www.TOWNSENDFABRICCUTTER.com

Dyes, hooks & supplies

W. Cushing & Company
PO Box 351
Kennebunkport, ME 04046
800-626-7847
customer@cushing.com
www.wcushing.com

Finishing supplies

(yarn and gold bent needle)
Needle Nook
100 East Main Street
Ligonier, PA 15658
724-238-7874
ndlnook@aol.com

Folk art

Findings
209 East Main Street
Ligonier, PA 15858
724-238-5252
khgreene@adelphia.net

Rusty Angel
4333 Route 30
Latrobe, PA 15650
724-532-1241

Frames

Morton Frame
311 Park Street
Winfield, KS 67156
620-221-1299
Country@kcisp.net

Nicholas Mosse pottery

Celtic Culture
218 West Main St.
Ligonier, PA 15658
724-238-2420
andrew_carr@celticcultureonline.com
www.celticcultureonline.com

Primitive patterns

Emma Lou's Primitives
2237 W. 124th St.
Leawood, KS 66209
913-469-4119

Tools & snippet baskets

Ault's Country Tyme
4515 Laser Road
Shelby, OH 44875
419-347-9957
lault@neo.rr.com

Wool supplies

Cotswold Woollen Weavers
Filkins, Nr Lechlade, Gloucestershire GL7 3JJ
England
From the US – 011-441-367-860491
Info@naturalbest.co.uk

Dorr Mill Store
PO Box 88
Guild, NH 0375 4
800-846-3677
dorrmillstore@sugar-river.net
www.dorrmillstore.com

The Wool Studio
Rebecca Erb
706 Brownsville Road
Sinking Spring, PA 19608
610 678 5448
rebecca@thewoolstudio.com
www.thewoolstudio.com

Woolley Fox preprinted patterns, books, hooks & supplies

Full-size patterns for the rugs shown in this book,
preprinted on rug backing of monk's cloth or
primitive linen, can be ordered via e-mail or by
phone from:
Woolley Fox LLC
132 Woolley Fox Lane
Ligonier, PA 15658
724-238-3600
woolleyfox@adelphia.net
www.woolleyfox.com

Note: The Woolley Fox very proudly owns the
patterns of Edyth O'Neill of Red Cape Rugs.